Advance Praise for
Memoirs of an Ordinary Guy

"Danny Olmes' folksy memoir packs a punch. He combines the wisdom gained from personal reflection with the lessons of an 'ordinary' American living through extraordinary times. He has written a sweet tale for the country he loves."
—MIRANDA DEVINE, *New York Post* columnist and author of *Laptop from Hell*

"Danny Olmes, a so-called 'ordinary guy,' has written an extraordinary book that offers countless life lessons the rest of us would be wise to heed and even emulate. Here's another important lesson: put this on your must-read list. Now."
—LEN SHAPIRO, longtime *Washington Post* sportswriter, columnist, and editor

"*Memoirs of an Ordinary Guy* is a unique and inspiring read. Penned in a series of vignettes, Danny captures the spirit of the 'Everyman' through introspective insights that will help readers contemplate the value of everyday experiences and living in the moment. Compassion for others and the importance of self are the essence of Danny's work and a must read for those seeking self-awareness and integration into a more rich and full life."

—Lt. Col. David Richardson, USMC, Ret. and author of *War Story*

"It has been my pleasure to see the development of Danny Olmes's thought-provoking book, *Memoirs of an Ordinary Guy*, from its very early stages to publication. Danny's goal has always been to capture life experiences that are not only meaningful to him but will also encourage readers to reflect on their own lives. Danny has succeeded in his objective, and I have no doubt that every reader will come away from this touching book with new perspectives on life."

—Chuck Cascio, longtime freelance writer and author of *The Fire Escape Stories* and six other books

MEMOIRS OF AN ORDINARY GUY

The Everyday Experiences
that Changed My Life

DANIEL STUART OLMES

Post Hill
PRESS

A POST HILL PRESS BOOK
ISBN: 978-1-63758-731-7
ISBN (eBook): 978-1-63758-732-4

Memoirs of an Ordinary Guy:
The Everyday Experiences that Changed My Life

Cover photo by Alice Quan
Cover design by Jacy Richardson

This is a work of nonfiction. All people, locations, events, and situation are portrayed to the best of the author's memory.

Post Hill Press
New York • Nashville
posthillpress.com

Published in the United States of America
1 2 3 4 5 6 7 8 9 10

To my children, Chase and Berkeley. You're the reason I know what love is. You're my kindred spirits and my guiding light, and you inspire me to be the greatest version of me. And the greatest version of me is actually you. I love you more than anything!

TABLE OF CONTENTS

FOREWORD

It's a rare thing indeed when someone tells you they are going to write a book and then actually completes the task. In my experience, writing a book is never easy. I've managed two. They often require more effort than their subject matter: in my case, climbing Mount Everest or traversing the Arabian Desert.

Danny has produced a heartfelt memoir and collection of short stories that chart his long road to contentment. These are enduring tales of the twists and turns of fate, and his central theme is taken right from the Declaration of Independence: the pursuit of happiness. What is it? How will I know when I find it? These and many more questions of faith and family took me back to some of the turning points in my own life. Danny promises to help us distinguish the good from the bad in our everyday experiences—and to cherish the former as a gift with divine provenance. I say Amen to that.

Even rarer than writing a book is actually appearing in the pages of a book you didn't write yourself! Danny has done me that great honor. He writes of the fire in his heart while listening to a Canadian wax lyrical on the subject of mountains and manifesting your own destiny. Clearly, that fire ştill burns for Danny. I am humbled to have played even the smallest part in helping him bring his stories into the world. They are worth the effort.

> - Jamie Clarke, adventurer, entrepreneur,
> and motivational speaker

AUTHOR'S NOTE

"And it is said that the Princess returned to her father's kingdom. That she reigned there with justice and a kind heart for many centuries. That she was loved by her people. And that she left behind small traces of her time on Earth, visible only to those who know where to look."

- Pan, Pan's Labyrinth

've always been an observer, an introvert. As a child—even today—I could look out the window for hours on long car rides and not say a word, perfectly content and deeply fixed on the simple and predictable landmarks of the typical American road trip: billboards without number, the rhythmic countdown of highway mile markers, the rotting barn perched on a rolling hillside, and the miles and miles of high-tension wires trailing off to a distant horizon.

And even though I saw the same things over and over—just ordinary things—they never seemed any less mysterious or any less worthy of my attention. There was always a subtle detail that required a more thoughtful examination. There was always something that made it impossible to look away. And there was always something more to learn. Maybe it's no coincidence that many years later I'd begin writing a book on the simple, everyday experiences that changed my life, and that, although I'm just an ordinary guy, I'm able to live an extraordinary life.

Every day, we encounter things that can inspire us to see the world a little differently, to take pause, to learn something new, or even to recognize the Divine. They can be a person, a memory, a character in a book, seven miles of asphalt, or even a can of Coke. They are anything and everything, and their gifts are many: a new perspective, a sense of peace, an important lesson, or perhaps a glimpse at another level of our being. They're a delicate reminder that there's always something beautiful to see, always something important to learn, and always a better way to live—a better version of ourselves. These experiences—the people and stories in this book—have brought me to a fuller understanding of what it means to be alive. They've been powerful guideposts in my life, and the most beautiful thing is that they're not unique. They're the experiences we all have, every day.

These stories have shown me the way—a path to the life I've always wanted. Over time, they continue to teach and inspire, and their lessons grow and evolve just as we all do. I look back on these people and events often, and they always have something more to tell. Their messages are timeless and can echo across our lives if we let them. As such, I chose to bring these stories to life through the one thing I know best:

the language of love. They're the history of my soul, and there's no greater privilege than to share them with you.

While reading this small book of short stories—all true events from my life—I hope you can relate to their simple messages, to the triumphs as well as the trials. I hope you'll be inspired to keep a similar record of your daily encounters, one that you can cherish throughout your life. I hope you find a new road, a new way to happiness that you didn't know before. And, most importantly, I hope something inside you changes forever, that your days from now on will be a little brighter, and that your personal journey will be lifted to the stars. The following pages are an invitation to be always mindful of the love and beauty around us every day. We just need to know where to look.

INTRODUCTION

"And above all, watch with glittering eyes the whole world around you because the greatest secrets are always hidden in the most unlikely places. Those who don't believe in magic will never find it."

- Roald Dahl

Okay. Bear with me here for a few pages. I know introductions are sometimes a chore when starting a new book, but it's important for me to say a few things first. It will help frame the purpose and motivation for this book and give me a chance to tell you a bit about myself—to set the stage for the greatest stories ever told, mine and yours.

First, thank you for your time. Time is precious. It's the commodity I think we can all agree—deep down—is the most sought after, the most coveted, and the most personal. It's a total cliché, but not many of us reach the end of our lives and wished we had more stuff. We wished we had more time, more moments. This book is about finding those moments. And given the value of time, I feel lucky and humbled to be able to share some of my moments with you. I'm grateful that this book of short stories is something you've chosen to spend your time with, and hopefully in reading my stories, they'll remind you of yours. Hopefully, they'll inspire you to see things you haven't seen before, the things that are right in front of us but oftentimes unnoticed. If I had to guess, these stories will probably sound familiar.

The following pages reveal some of my precious treasures, and I decided to bring these events to print because of the impact they've had on me. They've altered the course of my life. They've changed how I view the world. And they've reshaped my mindset in many ways. I hope they can do the same for you and that you'll feel inspired to take a similar accounting of your own experiences, to relive them, and to find the magic, so to speak.

These stories are of real events with real people, and they're written to stand alone and deliver simple messages. I've kept these accounts brief. They're not complicated because they're the everyday experiences we all have. But I'd like to take a few pages to tell you a bit about myself and to acknowledge some important things upfront. I'd like to place these stories in the context of my personal faith and perspectives. I'd like to acknowledge that I don't have all the answers. And I'd like to lend credence to the title of this book, that I'm just an ordinary guy bearing witness to the beauty of his experience—the experience we all share.

I believe intent is the key to most things in my life. It's important because it usually answers the question of why I do the things that I do. For example, it's one thing to do good and serve others, but why am I doing that? What is my intent? Is it to truly serve others? Or is it to serve myself, to show others how good I am? And if the underlying intent of my actions isn't pure, does that diminish their value? I believe it does, because poor intent rarely leads to something good. As a consequence, I've learned to place a high value on being well-intentioned, and my intent in these pages is to simply to make your world a little brighter; that through these stories you'll recall and find those in your own life, and that you'll ponder and care for them deeply.

It's not my intent to cast judgment on the state of the world. There's plenty of that around, and perhaps that's the problem. My hope, on some small level, is to fill the world with more love, one person and one story at a time. Success in this endeavor will be, as Ralph Waldo Emerson once said, "To appreciate beauty; to find the best in others; to leave the world a bit better...[and] to know even one life has breathed easier because you lived. This is to have succeeded." And I hope these stories and experiences inspire you to find and relive those in your own life, and that through them, you'll be transformed.

It's also important for me to acknowledge what I know I'm not. In his commencement address at the University of

Houston in 2016, Matthew McConaughey said this: "Look, the first step that leads to our identity in life is usually not, 'I know who I am.' That's not the first step. The first step is usually, 'I know who I am not.' Process of elimination. Defining ourselves by what we are not is the first step that leads us to really knowing who we are."

That quote makes sense to me. What am I *not*? It's a question that requires a routine and thorough self-assessment and a lifelong commitment to being true to myself. After all, my goal—and it's hard—is not to become what I'm not, but to become who I really am. So, what am I not? Well, I'm not trying to save the world. I'm not interested in fame or fortune. I'm not a prophet, and I'm not trying to be your guru. My only motivation *is* you, to change *your* world—to play a small role in your pursuit of happiness. I want you to find love and meaning in the world, just as I've found in my own life. This book is not a manual for happiness; it's a gift, a personal offering to those who'll accept it. If I've learned anything, it's gratitude, and I hope this book begins to repay an enormous debt I have with a world that has given me so much.

You won't hear me proclaim ultimate truths, or that one person is right and another is wrong. I've grown weary of this in my life. But I'll tell you what I believe and how I came to believe it. Belief is synonymous with faith—the absence of knowing. Socrates once said, "The only true wisdom is in knowing that you know nothing." A wise statement indeed and one that I've learned to embrace in my own life. Therefore, when I say, "I believe," it means it's something I feel strongly about, but not that "I know." There's only one thing I know for sure, and I'll discuss that later in this book (Chapter 11 – The Pearl).

I'll tell you about my experiences, those that have fundamentally changed my view of the world. I'll tell you what worked for me, but that won't necessarily work for everyone. What you do with this information is ultimately your choice and your responsibility. I'm not going to tell you how to live your life. I'm not going to preach. That wouldn't be the right thing to do.

So who am I? In truth, I'm just a regular guy. I try to not take myself too seriously. I coach my son's baseball teams. I grill hot dogs and hamburgers for Sunday barbecues. I watch football and mow the grass once a week. I say the F-word. I smoke a cigar occasionally. And I still listen to the Wu-Tang Clan at age forty-five (okay, maybe I'm not so ordinary). I am, by *most* standards, quite ordinary, but like I said in the author's note, I've learned how to live an extraordinary life. And as you'll see in the pages that follow, the extraordinary is there for all of us. It doesn't mean rich or famous. It doesn't mean better. To me, it means grateful, honest, happy, loving, fearless, and faithful.

A few years ago, I started writing some things down, a short list of experiences that I didn't want to forget. The things

I've written in this journal are not major milestones like my marriage, the birth of my children, or the death of a loved one. Those were too obvious and not easily forgotten. But every day, we have experiences that have the power to change our lives, even if they're quite ordinary. And once in a while, even the Divine is a detail of the daily.

For millennia, people of all faiths and traditions have believed that God walks among us. They've cherished the tender mercies that he leaves behind—the subtle reminders of his love for us and the power that faith and inspiration can have in the world. I wrote these things down because to lose this information would be a surrender of my testimony to our humanity and how we're blessed through other people. My purpose in these writings is simple: to share with you those journeys and experiences that have had a profound impact on me. But they might not be what you think. They're the things we most often miss, the miracles hiding in plain sight. Their lessons and messages can be life-altering if we choose to listen, and if we seek them out with a curious spirit.

It's in the subtlety of my everyday life where I find myself closest to God. This is where I believe love and compassion are in their purest and simplest form. Every day we're given glimpses of the Divine, small cracks in the doorways to eternity. They show up in countless ways: in our conversations with one another, in random photographs, in the people that pass by, in forgotten memories, and in friends and strangers alike. It took me a long time to realize this, and only when I slowed down and took a true account of the beauty around me was I able to hear the still, small voice of God and the delicate whisperings of the Holy Spirit. Every day since has been different. Where before I was dissatisfied and confused, I'm now content and at peace. Where before I was lost, I've now found something. Where before I searched for answers, now I know that the questions are just as important. I found that I only have two things: I have love and I have my choices.

I choose to believe that God walks beside each of us, that he resides in spirit form in everyone. I believe he's the inspiration for our general goodness as human beings, the embodiment of love, and the source of all that is; and it's our responsibility to recognize him when his hands are at work in the world. I choose to believe that he gave us the two greatest gifts in the universe: love and freedom. But with freedom comes an awesome responsibility and, by contrast, a terrible consequence. Love, too, is a function of that freedom. And that's why I believe there's nothing more important than our choices. They matter more than anything. And the ultimate choice—the most personal to every one of us—is how we choose to respond, in each moment, to the things we experience. Those choices become our experience; they become our lives. How we respond defines each moment, and the collection of those moments is what we call life.

I believe opposition is necessary, but it's mostly of our own creation and its extent, too, is a matter of choice. Without question, there's an obvious and sometimes painful unfairness of human life: the disparity of the rich and poor, racial and gender injustice, the untimely loss of a loved one, mental illness, addiction, famine, disease, wars, and natural disasters. The examples are endless, and so many things in life seem beyond our control or understanding. But it's the world we live in and the life we have. We must accept that, and regardless of what happens to us, regardless of the conditions we face, we can always choose how we respond. Obviously, that choice can be incredibly difficult depending on the circumstance, but that freedom is rarely, if ever, taken away.

I believe that evil and suffering are many times a natural consequence of that freedom, and, as a species, we've often chosen poorly. Hardship seems endemic to our way of life, but it's also, I believe, not a good reason to reject a benevolent and loving creator and our union with the absolute. I believe that our creator doesn't allow us to suffer. He allows us to live. As a consequence, I believe the only way to truly understand and appreciate love is to also experience a lack of it. We're designed to learn by experience, both good and bad, and through each other—the greatest teachers we'll ever have.

Why am I saying all this? Well, it's because I recognize that life's not fair, it doesn't treat all of us equally, bad things happen, and "Life is difficult." This was the first sentence of

M. Scott Peck's famous book *The Road Less Traveled*. He said the road to spiritual growth is a long one, and I believe that. I believe, however, that we can be gently guided along this road through our faith, through the simple experiences we have day-to-day, and through each other.

I've had some difficult periods in my life. From one lonely day many years ago, I had to battle back from within an inch of my life. On that day, everything changed: every relationship, every goal, and every dream. When I was twenty-eight years old and prior to most of the events described in this book, I had to start over. A new man needed to be built from the ground up. It was difficult. In the end, however, a choice was made to live on and to live well. That said, I fully acknowledge that my problems are just the dreams of many, that my worst days are probably ones that others can only hope for.

I don't know what it feels like to lose a child. I don't know what it feels like to live in extreme poverty. I don't know what it feels like to suffer from mental illness. And I don't know what it feels like to be at the unceasing will of a merciless torturer. I've drawn a couple lucky cards from the deck of life, and I'm grateful for all the opportunities and advantages I've had. I'm grateful, too, for the disadvantages and pain that I haven't experienced. Some might even say that I've lived a privileged life. That's probably true. I've been given a great deal, but that also means I need to give something back. I hope this book is that gift.

Even so, I expect that many readers will see the words and stories in this book as somewhat naïve, even foolishly optimistic. I acknowledge that your response may be, "Well, it's easy for you to say!" That's true. It's easy for me to say, "Just choose to be happy." It's easy for me to say, "Take account of your experiences and you'll be happy." I understand it's not that simple, and we're all different. All I'm saying is that, regardless of what happens to you, it's your choice how to respond. There's enough beauty and love in the world for us all to find joy and happiness, to find a reason to be happy as opposed to being unhappy, frustrated, and dissatisfied. How we view the world is almost always a choice. And where we lack understanding and hope, maybe that's where faith takes over.

These writings are a record of some of the greatest events of my life, those that have brought me to a fuller understanding of my soul and the God that created it. For many years, though, faith was elusive, my creator hidden. He remained hidden because I had false expectations. I expected to be given the keys to the Kingdom. I expected knowledge that I wasn't designed to know or even understand. I expected prayers to be answered on my terms, for my problems to magically disappear. I expected to talk to God face-to-face, and when I did, I'd make my case that he was wrong and I was right. My ability to follow—to believe—was overcome by my arrogance. Ironically, what I sought was antithetical to a life of faith, the one thing I wanted most. And faith is the ultimate choice: what do we choose to believe?

I've chosen a path of discovery, a passionate dance through the great unknown. I've learned to embrace and enjoy the struggle, and I fear nothing because I believe God is in everything. I believe there's an underlying order of things, a reality I'll one day understand. I believe love is the language of God and, as a single embrace in everything, is the key to our happiness in this life.

Mark Twain once wrote: "The two most important days in your life are the day you are born and the day you find out why." These stories are my why, the people in them my teachers. And in many ways, they answer the greatest question of all—what is my purpose in this life? I believe that once you recognize and compose your own stories, you'll also find your why. You'll never again walk alone. You'll have a newfound perspective and find a deeper love in your heart. You'll discover that God lives inside every one of us. And you'll find the magic. This is my invitation. This is my promise.

I'll start this journey in Chapter 1 by describing an event that inspired me to write this book. Then I'll take you through a dark period in my life, but one marked by personal triumph. A turning point in this dark period—Chapter 2—was a dream, one that gave me a clear warning that I'd luckily heed with caution and a sense of urgency. In the next two chapters, I'll tell a couple extraordinary stories—real events—that, while contrary to the main theme of this book, inspired me to think a little differently. They kept me alive and taught me to see things in my life with a renewed energy and spirit.

From that point forward and for the remainder of this book, I'll tell you about the little things, the everyday experiences and people—many times strangers—who changed my life. As with life, there is no need to rush when reading this book. This is my story, but I hope it will remind you of yours and that it'll inspire in you a different view of the world and tell the human story we all share.

CHAPTER 1

THE MOUSE

"A single mom who's working two jobs and still finds time to take her kid to soccer practice, that's a miracle. A teenager who says 'no' to drugs and 'yes' to an education, that's a miracle. People want Me to do everything for them. But what they don't realize is they have the power. You want to see a miracle, son? Be the miracle."

- God (Morgan Freeman), Bruce Almighty

I love to read. But it's not something that I was particularly good at for a long time. It's something I struggled with for many years. I enjoyed learning, but to focus on sentence after sentence was always tough for me. I still have challenges taming my wandering mind. Background noise—like a TV or a conversation of any kind—is usually too much. And yet, it's funny how sometimes assumed weaknesses eventually become lifelong passions. To read is to explore, and as such, there are countless journeys we can take in the form of the written word. And they cost almost nothing.

There are many genres in my Kindle library: fiction, non-fiction, history, alternate history, religion, spirituality, and New Age. But physics, in particular, is a subject I find fascinating. I'd say it has become a hobby, but I also have to admit that I'm quite a hack by most standards. In truth, I understand very little of what I read (about physics). And given my lack of formal education on the subject, my hobby—my investigation—is mainly reduced to impressions. What does this material mean in the end? What is it telling us about the world we live in? What does it mean to me and my life?

Quantum mechanics, a discrete branch of physics, is the science of the subatomic world and is by far the most successful theory and mathematical framework in history. Initially developed in the early twentieth century, its equations are some of the most accurate in modern science and have withstood the test of time and technological innovation. Without quantum theory, we wouldn't have iPhones, pharmaceuticals, the internet, or really anything with an electronic circuit. The theory describes the physical and behavioral properties of nature at the scale of atoms and subatomic particles and, without getting too technical, paints a picture of reality that is completely counterintuitive to how we experience life as human beings. Examples include wave-particle duality, quantum scenarios where effects precede causes, faster-than-light communication, subatomic particles being in superposition (two places at once), and the fact that observation alone can influence the physical world. Each of these examples violate either common sense or any known laws of physics. To quote one of the pioneers of quantum theory, Richard Feynman: "I believe it's safe to say that no one understands quantum mechanics." And to date, no one truly does. Scientists can predict with incredible accuracy the function of the subatomic world, yet we have no clue what it really means.

Often absent in the analysis of quantum mechanics, too, is an attempt by scientists to address the underlying philosophy. It's one thing to understand how a particular system works, but *why* it works that way is another question entirely. What is the data telling us about the nature of our reality? At a fundamental level—on the smallest scales—what are we really made of, and is there something else that we can't see?

Scientists usually steer away from the philosophy of physics, as it's considered by most to be metaphysics and beyond proof and testability. That said, I believe physics points to, as Albert Einstein once said, "something deeply hidden." It hints at a fundamental reality that is purposely or, through our designed limitations as human beings, veiled from our common experience and shrouded even from our most precise and complex machines. Our best guesses about the true nature of the world are theoretical—and in themselves metaphysics—with very little hope of ever being tested in a laboratory.

I choose to believe physics is telling us that the world we see (or the world we think we see) is so utterly complex, so counterintuitive, and so mind-numbingly large that it was *designed* to remain a mystery. It was designed so faith and free will would be preserved in the absence of our understanding. I believe God is present in all the awesome wonder of nature but remains hidden so that we may walk a life of faith. Cal Tech physicist and best-selling author Sean Carroll said: "Our experience of the world, which is confined to an extraordinarily tiny fraction of reality, doesn't leave us well-equipped to think in appropriate ways about the question of its existence."

The questions are usually the big three: *Where did we come from? What is our purpose? Where are we going?* (or more bluntly) *What happens when we die?* Science, broadly speaking, has produced some of our greatest accomplishments as a species. It's in our essential nature to explore and discover new things, and I personally believe it's an important use of our time and resources. And yet, after centuries of inquiry (and one hundred years since the equations of quantum theory were first developed) and through our collective intelligence, we're simply no closer to answering those big questions. In fact, our most successful theories to describe the world around us—general relativity for the large-scale objects we see every day and quantum mechanics for the subatomic world—are so mathematically incompatible with one another that, when combined to describe a unified picture of reality, they yield results that border on the absurd. Curiously, their results are infinity, something the human brain and our best equations can't seem to handle. If science can't answer those questions, then who will? Maybe answers aren't what we really need. Maybe we just need each other.

Despite my love of science, I'm also a man of faith. I believe in the gospel story of Jesus Christ. I believe in his ministry here on Earth. I believe in the message of love and forgiveness, and I understand my responsibility as his disciple. I also believe there are many paths to God. As they say in Islam, there's no god but God, and I believe he is equally manifest in all of us. I believe he's come to Earth many times, in different ways to different people. And whether it be paradise, nirvana, enlightenment, salvation, grace, or mercy that we seek, I believe we're all using different words to describe the same thing, the infinite oneness of the Divine—the infinity that our best equations seem to reveal.

At the time of this writing—Summer 2020—I'm forty-two years old. I live in a beautiful little home in Northern Virginia with my wife and two children. I'm the co-founder of a technology start-up and eagerly beginning a new career as a writer. I'm comfortable in my own skin, and faith and spirituality continue to be my guide. But the road to now wasn't easy, and I'm grateful for the experiences that have led me to this point, including the wonderful people I've met along the way. I'm certainly not without my flaws, but I can honestly say that I'm comfortable with the unknown, excited by change, and at peace with the world and my creator. But for many years, this wasn't the case. I just didn't get it. In many ways, I was dissatisfied, intellectually arrogant, and spiritually lost. But a totally random encounter ten years ago changed all of that; it was a discovery that would fundamentally alter my view of the world.

On a day like any other, I was backing into a space in my parking garage at work. As I did so, an elderly woman with a Mickey Mouse shirt slowly walked by the front of my car. Her body was somewhat curled up. She was frail and moved with inordinate difficulty. Her skin was cratered and blemished, and I could see her pale, grayish scalp through her wiry and thinning hair. She was easily ninety years old. But in her hand was an object that would redefine my attitude forever—a gym bag. I thought physics was the way to understanding our world until I saw that old woman in the parking garage.

I was stunned by the scene in front of me, the physical and spiritual endurance of this woman. It gave me the chills— beyond chills, actually. It was a deeply resonant and harmonic vibration from head to toe, waves of energy and love sent right to my core. The energy was so powerful I could almost hear it. But, most importantly, I could feel it, and it felt different. It felt like God. Pure, simple, absolute. It felt like a message, and sitting there, I just knew that I was in the midst of something great, something fundamental. In an instant, I saw an answer to the question I sought most: *What is my purpose?* Clearer to me than anything I knew to that point, I realized that I had uncovered one of the greatest clues to life itself—at least in mine anyway. The answer was crystal clear: my purpose was the deliberate and daily pursuit of the Divine, and with an ageless spirit and a renewed curiosity, I could see God in simple ways. It was confirmed to me that, if I could have this experience with a total stranger on a random and otherwise average day, I could have such an experience again, and again, and again, every day, with anyone and anything.

It was revealed to me that there is a profoundly higher source of love that surrounds us every day, and that source can be our guiding light. It can make the unbearable bearable. It can clear the confusion. It can offer faith to the faithless. In short, it can make miracles happen. But what I realized, too, is that miracles are mostly of our own making. We create the miracle. I also realized in that moment that energy and age aren't mutually exclusive, and I promised myself to never compromise the pursuit of knowledge and never surrender my passion for exploration and personal discovery—a manner on which I so diligently thrived as a young person.

I'd embark on an honest pursuit of true experiences—my goal, to achieve spiritual endurance and growth and, regardless of my age, I committed to never leaving my gym bag behind; the spiritual workout is continuous and lifelong. It was the beginning of a spiritual transformation for me, an unexpected shift from the material to the ethereal and from the physical to the metaphysical. In the basement of a dingy parking garage on just an average day, I found what I wanted—the beginning of a journey to personal enlightenment. I never wanted dogma. I just wanted faith. I wanted peace. And I found it with Mickey Mouse and an old woman I never met—someone I'd never see again.

With a wry smile, I realized—triumphantly—I'd never find that answer in any of my physics books and, while they remain fascinating, I'd start to also learn from a different resource. My spiritual progression would be rooted in the ordinary, everyday experiences that are accessible in every moment. I'd come to understand the eternal code of the universe is written in a language we can all understand: the simple language of love. And that eternal code—the promise from above (or maybe from within)—is written into every one of our stories, from beginning to end. And on that glorious day, I decided to keep a journal of my stories. Years later, I'd be inspired to start sharing them with you. They'd become the *Memoirs of an Ordinary Guy*.

There's nothing more beautiful than a curious spirit, and I choose to believe we're placed in a great unknown by design, to walk in faith versus omniscience, and to walk with one another. There's nothing that makes our creator prouder than for his children to find the miracles in the mystery and meaning in the mundane. *You can be the miracle.* Miracles surround us every day. They're the people we share this life with, and they're the experiences in our lifelong walk from here to there.

They can be our guides and our teachers if we let them. They can be the waymakers.

As a child, I looked to the heavens to find God. I looked up and out. But after seeing Mickey Mouse that morning, I realized he might be walking right in front of me. And as Jesus said to his disciples at the Last Supper, "On that day you'll realize that I am in my Father, and you are in me, and I am in you." (John 14:20)

On that day, I realized the Divine is in all of us, and the Lord is alive in everyone. I realized there were eight billion manifestations of him on Earth, and eight billion opportunities to seek him out. I realized I could see God without actually seeing God, and while my body is temporary, my soul is eternal, and I'd never be too old to wear a Mickey Mouse shirt.

My dear friends, I promise that if you can find God on the margins, if you have the patience and humility to look when most others look away, and if you can pay attention to what's quietly dancing in the shadows, then you'll begin to rewrite your story, and it will change your life.

CHAPTER 2

THE DREAM

"I should be loyal to the nightmare of my choice. I was anxious to deal with this shadow by myself alone—and to this day I don't know why I was so jealous of sharing with any one the peculiar blackness of that experience."

- Joseph Conrad, Heart of Darkness

What happens when we dream? Where do we go? Nobody knows for sure. Dreams are a curious phenomenon. Enigmatic. Bizarre. And most of the time, we overlook the experience of dreaming—an often-forgotten encounter with another world. But maybe dreams can provide a hint of something deeper? Maybe they're a telltale journey into the bottomless caverns of our mind and soul. They can be as much an affirmation as they are a warning.

We all have dreams. And they have many moods: tense, terrifying, depressing, baffling, blurry, mysterious, exhilarating, emotional, spiritual, uplifting, sexual, sensual, adventurous, vivid, fleeting. Some dreams we remember. Most we don't. But this one I remember. I've remembered it above all others. Its message—its warning, as I've come to realize—was one of the greatest of my life. Intensely personal, yet universal. A moment in time, yet timeless. Secular, yet spiritual. This dream occurred at a low point in my life, in a period of darkness. It occurred during a confusing time, when it was difficult to understand who I was or where I was going. I've kept this to myself for many years and I don't know why, but it's the nightmare of my choice. Perhaps better said, it's the nightmare of my choices. And I've remained loyal to this day.

It's dark. Dark in every direction. Some sort of room. But it's not a room. No walls. No ceiling. Just dark. Hollow. Vacant. No depth. No contrast. No surfaces. No corners. Just darkness. No location. No space. No time. No sound. I'm nowhere. I'm alone. Lost. A sea of nothingness. Disoriented. Anxious. But not scared. Curious. Trying to see something. Trying to sense something. But nothing. Can't feel anything. Nothing to touch. Nothing to taste. Nothing to smell. Just looking. But nothing to look at. Nothing to see. But it's me. I know I'm here. It's like a fog. The fog is dark. No emotion. No spirit. Numb. No energy. No warmth. Nowhere to go. Nothing at all. It's a void. Outer space? No stars. Gravity. Feel heavy. Something pulling. My chest. Smothered. A prison? No bars. But restrained. Contained. More pressure now. Standing. But no ground. No floor. I look to my right and then look back. It's there.

A new friend hangs in the abyss. On a black wire. Hanging from nowhere. A light bulb. It's small. Clear. Strings. Filaments. I can see them. Strings of light. Strings of hope. Still confused. A dim and ominous light descends. Fills the room. Can't penetrate the darkness. Still dark. But I'm somewhere now. Less anxious. Still curious. Waiting. Wondering. A few objects come to life. The mist is lifting. The room starts to glow. A greenish tint. Almost grey. I'm seeing more clearly now. More gravity. A floor. I look down. Cracking cement. Grey. Now a smell. It smells old. Cold. Musty. Damp. A basement? Underground? No one around. Only my friend. I look up. The light. I look down. Now something else. Right in front of me. It wasn't there before. Now it is. Just under the light. A plastic table. Small. Rectangular. Nothing on it. Two metal chairs. Across from each other. Facing each other. The chairs are pulled out. Ready to be seated. A table for two? But who else? Still alone. An interview? An interrogation? I don't know.

A figure now. Walking toward me. Blurry. A dark blue aura. Some white. Glowing. Vibrating. I can feel it. A presence. My stomach drops. Sharp pain. Churning. Uncertain. Afraid. A cold chill runs through my body. Almost electric. Anxiety returns. Can't escape. The figure feels evil. It feels bad. Sinister. Fear now. Clearer now. It's a man. Thin. Strong. Jeans. White T-shirt. Is it me? Looks like me. Only different. He moves slowly. Methodically. Confidently. Demonically. A predator. A hunter. He sits down. I don't want to look. I know it's bad. Don't want to see. I look. Crystal clear. I step back. Startled. Shocked. He's disfigured. Ugly.

Horrible. Evil. Twisted. Intimidating. Ghostly. Primal. Mouth open. Grinning. Baring his teeth. Sharp teeth. Eyes burning. Seething. Determined. Intent on my pain. Intent on my fear. Intent on my hatred. He's me. My creation. My fault. I'm to blame. Only one to blame. Don't want to be him. The enemy. Want to leave. Vulnerable. Alone. No one to help. He looks at me. I look away. I can't look. Scared now. Terrified. I can't hide. No options. I need help. But I have to face him. I know I have to. Can't avoid it. Can't run away. I look up slowly. Now eye-to-eye. Locked. Committed now. He says, "Sit down."

No choice. Can't delay. Something needs to change. I sit down. He sits. Still starting. A long pause. An eternity. He wants me to look. He wants me to acknowledge. He wants me to see his face. Craving fear. My demise. He wants me to say something. I say nothing. Silent. Frozen. He leans forward and says, "I'm going to destroy you now." Something takes hold. Something different. An odd sensation now. A wave. A stillness. Focus. Power. Adrenaline. Tingling. Haven't felt it for a long time. New strength. Prepared. Confident. Stoic. No fear. I don't know why. Something changed. What changed? Should be scared. But I'm not. It's love. I feel the light. It feels warm. Comfort. Finally. Something in my right hand now. Confidence builds. I smile. More warmth. Radiating. Powerful. In control. Still tingling. Anticipation builds. Can't wait for what's next. Future uncertain. But confident. Present. Feeling again. What's in my hand? It's cool. Almost cold. Smooth. Heavy. But lighter than usual. It's metal. Rubber. Grooves massaging my fingers. Three fingers. Perfect fit. Like a glove. There's something else. Pressure. My index finger. Something small. Delicate. Light. Cool. A gentle tap. I feel it. A trigger. My .44 Magnum. Game over. I can fight back. I can defend myself. Hope regained. One more thing. My thumb. I know what to do. I cock the hammer. The wheel spins. Counter clock. One click. No fear. But he's still there. Still evil. Overwhelming. He's confident. Ready to destroy me. Wants to. Wants nothing more. Destroying life. But only if I let him. The choice is mine. Table turned. Game changed. Advantage. I have it. He doesn't know it. But I do. Have what I need. Can defend myself. I raise the gun. Now a new feeling. More confidence. More power. A reckoning. But I don't need it. It doesn't work that way. I have another weapon. Another way. A better way. I place the gun on the table. Three words. Only three. I say, "Then go ahead."

He doesn't say a word. Doesn't hesitate. Picks it up. Ready to kill. He stands. I'm still sitting. Looking up. The light is there. Always will be. "Thank you, my friend." But I'm still the target. Always will be. Gun pointed. At my head. I see the sights. The barrel. The wheel. Hammer still cocked. But it's missing something. Something important. Six critical parts. It won't work without them. I know it. He doesn't. It's the key. Finally. He thinks it's finished. Accomplished. He thinks he won. He smiles. I smile back. Face-off. Eye-to-eye. Fight the good fight. The constant fray. The never-ending fight. With a new weapon. The right choices. It's all about choices. I know that now. No fear. He says nothing. Not another word. Pulls the trigger.

[click].

My eyes slam open.

CHAPTER 3

THE YELLOW BRICK ROAD

"In a word, to let the spiritual,
unbidden and unconscious,
grow up through the common.
This is to be my symphony."

- William Henry Channing

The dream was a premonition, a sign of things to come, and it was from there that I began to wander through another confusing and difficult period in my life. I was twenty-seven years old, single, and living at home was not a "place" I wanted to be. I'd purchased a new-construction condominium in Reston, Virginia a couple years earlier, but it was overdue on delivery, and I was just biding my time to finally move out on my own. I was trying to "save some money," or so I told myself and others. Sound familiar? But I wasn't in a good place. I was in a spiritual and emotional hole, and I needed someone to help me crawl out, but no one came to my aid. The only thing that seemed to come was more frustration. I was patiently waiting for something—anything—to go my way, and life seemed very unclear. I was also patiently seeking something else, a faith in God. That was the missing piece—something I desperately wanted and needed—but I had absolutely no clue where to begin.

My faith journey wasn't starting off well, but how could I have guessed that Elton John would be the last person I'd hear from before the most important thirty seconds of my life? Given an event of such magnitude, I thought the soundtrack would've been a little more dramatic—"Enter Sandman," "Lose Yourself," "Carmina Burana." But that's not the way it happened. It was "Tiny Dancer."

At that time, I felt very much like a male version of Dorothy from *The Wizard of Oz*. I was lost in a foreign world over which I had little control, chased by an ominous force intent on my continued fear and confusion, and I was unsure how I'd ever get home or find a sense of normal in my life. I was hopelessly trolling the yellow brick road in search of direct answers to life's mysteries, in search of a solution to my daily frustrations and perceived miseries. I convinced myself there was an Emerald City out there somewhere, and I was on a tireless pilgrimage to learn from its masters. *If I could just get there*, I said to myself, *things would be better*. I thought I could find God somewhere inside the city's walls, and when I found him, he'd let me in on all the secrets, as if I had a privileged place in the faith journey we all walk, like it was some kind of destination.

It was a frustrating and fruitless journey, trying to develop a personal relationship with God. A personal relationship with God? What was that? I heard people say it all the time, but I never knew what it really meant. To me, it seemed like a cosmic carrot, dangled just out of reach. It felt like a hook, a scam. As a newcomer to faith, I was either on a fool's errand or I was the obstinate fool; I couldn't decide which. And despite my best efforts, I just wasn't getting anywhere, most likely due to the attitude I just described.

I was almost ready to give up. But then, along the yellow brick road, on a random night like any other, I got my first peek at the "man behind the curtain"—a flash of the ethereal, a postcard from the edge, a tiny droplet from the Source. Although agnostic in its religious overtone, this experience would later form the basis of my Christian faith and my beginning as a follower of Jesus Christ. This experience would also keep my heart and mind open to other traditions and paths to God, as its likeness would parallel many similar accounts I would read in the years to come. It was a simple, pure, astonishing event, and one, I believe, we all have access to. It was a source of Divine energy, one that had laid dormant inside me for too many years. In a few words, I'll try to bring it back to life.

When I was twenty-seven years old, I found myself at the tail end of a consulting contract in the financial industry and also in the death grip of an alcohol problem. Luckily, I wasn't a daily drinker. I never felt physically addicted to alcohol. In truth, I didn't even like the way it made me feel. It's likely I dodged a bullet there, that perhaps my recovery was eased a bit by acknowledging my problem early on. But it was something I did way too much. I was generally bored and dissatisfied with life, and a drink made all that go away. Lots of people drink, but I drank differently, with no off switch. Once I started, it was very difficult to stop, and this led to weekend after weekend of binge drinking until I passed out, followed by several blurry days of recovery and then back at it again. Life, as they say in twelve-step programs, had become unmanageable, and this cascade of ups and downs—this parasite—was eating away at me mentally and spiritually. I was on a collision course with irreversible consequence. And the sad part was, I didn't have a reason to stop. That all started to change on the night of July 15, 2005—the night I asked God for a most unusual favor.

Rewind one year. Bored one Sunday the previous summer, I found myself at a local driving range. Golf is a passion of mine, but on that particular day, something was very different. Each swing seemed harder than the one before it, each strike of the ball less satisfying. I started to feel an odd sense of disorientation, like when you begin to feel lost in a place you've never been before. Except that day, I was lost in a place I'd been hundreds of times. I had no idea where I was, but I knew for sure it was not where I wanted to be.

As I hit my last shot, I came to a definite pause, one I'd remember for the rest of my life. In the heat of the afternoon sun, with my left hand on my hip and my right hand gently resting on my eight-iron like a cane, I raised my focus to the horizon and then slowly hung my head in surrender. It was a moment that eerily paralleled the iconic scene from *Star Wars: Episode IV – A New Hope* when Luke Skywalker gazes across a barren desert to the dually setting suns of Tatooine, unsure of his purpose and immediate future. A most humble and honest smirk pursed my lips, and with a slight shake of my head, I acknowledged, for the first time, that my life wasn't headed in the right direction. It was the first time I admitted that I was lost, and I knew something had to change. Alone in the heat and sweat of an August day, I realized I had to become someone different; I wasn't the man I wanted to be.

Then, for whatever reason, I felt a strong desire to leave. This would've normally been unusual, but something was urging me to go. And just as Luke Skywalker curiously peered over the horizon to that triumphant "Force Theme" by John Williams, I raised my head back up, tapped my eight-iron on the mat with a dubious confidence, and handed my bucket of balls to the gentlemen next to me. Then I got in my car and headed off to the grocery store. I didn't need groceries. I didn't even know what I was going to buy, but that's where I felt I needed to go. Ten minutes later, I was at a local Safeway—rather ironic looking back, because it was the safe way I'd eventually find.

To make a long story short, this seemingly random trip to the grocery store led me to a chance encounter with an old friend, then back to church, to a small Bible study, and finally, at the conclusion of one summer evening a year later, into a deep personal prayer asking God to test me and that I was ready to receive his will in my life. It was a request of faith and a statement of surrender; faith, that I could handle the challenges that lay ahead, whatever they may be, and surrender, that I'd finally allow someone else to help guide my path. It was an odd request, to be tested. I was losing control of my life and, yet, my first instinct was to be tested more. Hadn't I already gone through enough? Was it someone else's time to take over? Did I need to be shown the bottom in order to rise up once again?

On my way home from Bible study that night, Elton John's "Tiny Dancer" began playing on my car stereo. I was immediately reminded of a wonderful scene from the movie *Almost Famous*, where a group of rock stars is heading off in their tour bus after a night of excessive partying and particularly poor behavior by their lead guitarist. The scene is a bit tense and subdued from the awkwardness of the night before, but then one of the band members gently taps the lead guitarist on the shoulder. It was a silent way of saying, "Don't worry. Everything's okay. We still love you." Another member of the band notices this and then starts singing the lyrics to "Tiny Dancer," which is now playing in background. One by one, all the band members join in, and the mood immediately changes—intense joy and camaraderie filling the scene. Then the lead character, a high school boy who's writing a story for *Rolling Stone* and long overdue in his time with the band, says to a groupie played by Kate Hudson, "I need to go home." She gently hushes him and says, "You are home." I remember feeling an intense desire to be home again, to be connected to the world I lived in, something that had been absent for so long. I remember feeling a lack of joy. And then someone tapped me on the shoulder.

The next thirty seconds I can only describe as a total rush—a mystical roller-coaster ride through the previously unknown. From the deepest parts of my soul, waves of intense light and energy began radiating throughout my body. My perception of time, distance, and space disappeared, and a pure love vibrated through every nerve ending in my body. I was completely free of pain or worry, both empty and full at the same time—for the first time. For that brief period, I felt like the center of the universe, connected to the source of all that is. The vastness of the moment seemed infinite, a dimension with no physical boundaries. I was finally with God. I was home.

But the more and more I tried to hold on, the more I felt him slip back behind the curtain. This feeling eventually drifted off, and I arrived home with a pleasant yet pessimistic curiosity. But when I went to bed that night, the questions didn't stop: What just happened? Was that my imagination? Was that an experience my brain created because I needed it? Or was it something else entirely? Eventually I drifted off to sleep that night like most others, tired and genuinely not looking forward to another day like the one previous. But when I woke up that next morning, everything was different. My body felt lighter, my mind clearer. Sunlight shining between the leaves on the trees looked more beautiful than ever before, the colors so vivid and bright. The otherwise hectic and confusing world seemed calm and clear. It was like I'd finally awoken from a nightmare only to realize it was a dream—a dream come true.

That same day, I'd be oddly inspired to spend several hours behind a computer writing my first statement of faith. I'd be baptized for the second time a couple months later, and my faith journey seemed, in a short period, to take a big leap forward. But just like the pride before the fall or the calm before the storm, the real monster was lurking right around the corner. My true test, the one I asked God for at Bible study on an otherwise average summer evening, lay just ahead.

In writing this story, I remember something I said to one of my best friends in college: "When this stuff [alcohol] starts to affect who I am…I'll give it up for good." The few months following my baptism, I can only describe as a complete loss of control, a downward spiral that nearly ended my life. And after three trips to the emergency room as well as a short stay at a drug and alcohol treatment center near my home in Northern Virginia, I kept that promise to my friend. On January 21, 2006, I made a decision. I set out on a new course, the new direction that was so crystal clear on that day at the driving range. I took a left turn when I had previously turned right. It was the toughest and easiest decision I'd ever made.

Many of my relationships would change permanently, and for a period of time, my life was quite lonely. The healing process was straightforward, boring, and deliberate; full of mystery, uncertainty, and many times pain. But it was beautiful. It was the most real experience I'd ever had and one I wouldn't trade for anything. Every day following that cold and dreary day in January has been better than the one before it. This was new to me, and it was a miracle.

Many times, our prayers aren't answered in the way we want. I spent a lot of my life searching for something that wasn't actually "out there." I blamed everyone else for the things that weren't right in my life and I thought that I was living without, but after that experience in my car, I finally realized that most of what I need comes from within. There's truly no place like home, and I believe our home is the eternal ground—the basic and divine element from which we are made. The eternal ground is the infinite love, grace, and charity of God. He's the man behind the curtain and the conductor of that brilliant symphony to the auspicious melody of "Tiny Dancer." He is in me and I am in Him. We are one. He is one in all of us.

In the end, the mythical emerald city of Oz was not someplace "out there." It was inside me all along—deep below the surface—eagerly awaiting my arrival. The yellow brick road was only a detour, a short trip to a place I knew I didn't want to be. But it was a road I needed to take. Its lessons were countless and necessary. Thank you, Sir Elton! But now I have to say "Goodbye Yellow Brick Road." I was brought home by the ultimate waymaker—the God with whom I now have a personal relationship—the One inside me.

Miracles do happen. I now have the life I've always wanted. I'm becoming the man I want to be, and I have a wife and two children who are the most beautiful things I've ever seen. But I had to go through hell first. There had to be some tough days, and to quote one of my favorite songs, "Some Nights," by the band Fun., some "terrible nights."

CHAPTER 4

THE SHIMMER

"The effect of this cannot be understood without being there. The beauty of it cannot be understood, either, and when you see beauty in desolation it changes something inside you."

- Jeff VanderMeer, Annihilation

A s my drinking career was winding down, I definitely had "some terrible nights," but I'll always remember two in particular. On the two worst days of my life, the same thing happened, something beautiful. I caught a "fleeting glimpse"—an experience no wisdom of mine could possibly explain. And it wasn't "...out of the corner of my eye" as Pink Floyd describes in their famous song "Comfortably Numb." These two experiences were front and center, and I experienced them with a visceral clarity, something so alien at the time. I was uncomfortably numb, and contrary to the main theme of this book—the power of the ordinary, everyday experiences we all share—these two experiences were anything but ordinary. They were extraordinary, and they're part of my story.

These two events were separated by many months. They took place in completely different locations and they occurred without any obvious cause or announcement. They sort of just happened; I looked up, and they were there. The likeness of each was identical, and they came to me in the middle of the night, at two points where I felt the most alone in my life. I've never told this story before, and by all standards of normal, these two experiences are completely abnormal, unbelievable, and even a bit crazy. But I wasn't alarmed. I wasn't scared. They were oddly familiar, and they brought me more comfort than I could've ever possibly imagined.

On January 21, 2021—at age forty-three—I celebrated a major milestone in my life: fifteen years sober. That day, fifteen years earlier, was day one of my sobriety. To me, fifteen was always the magic number—the day I could say, "I haven't had a drink in fifteen years…" was also the day I could confidently say, "I beat it." Fifteen years, and it would be part of my past—forever. Fifteen years, and the greatest of all filters—time itself—would have succeeded in putting all the regret, all the personal anguish, and all the wasted life in the rearview mirror. Today I'm free. Today the future is bright, and I hope to live many more days and welcome each one with a breath of fresh air. But on these two days, I was totally alone. No one knew where I was or even the true extent of my problem. And pardon the physics reference, but there was a black hole in the middle of my chest, consuming all the light that I had. I was tiptoeing on the event horizon—the point of no return—and I wasn't even sure there'd be a tomorrow.

DAY ONE

Beep. Beep. Beep. Beep. Beep. I looked over. A flickering of peaks and valleys on a digital monitor. Something dripping from a plastic bag above. Wires. Tubes. Sharply descending into my body. The sound is even, methodical. Terrifying. Foreign. But it sounds better than I feel. My heart is racing. A feeling of dread. Doom. Crushing anxiety. I can't breathe. Heavy, forced. A grinding of teeth. Gnashing even. Clenched hands. Trembling. Out of life. Is this the end? The world is closing in around me. I want it to stop. I want to escape. I'm hot. I'm cold. Sweating. Shaking. Blurry. Fuzzy. I can't even think. But racing thoughts. Looking back and forth across the room, I search for something, anything. A sign of normal, a sign of hope. But nothing. A cold tile floor. White walls. Nothing. Sterile. I'm alone. No one's here. Maybe I want it that way. How did I get here? I know how. No excuses. No time left for excuses. It's all my fault. No one else's. It's on me now. My choices.

It was a cold, grey fall morning, and I'd just checked myself into a drug and alcohol treatment facility in Northern Virginia. I'd been drinking around the clock for a week, had barely eaten for days, and was twenty pounds underweight. I'd already been to the emergency room twice in the previous three months for alcohol related issues, mainly "severe dehydration" or "potential alcohol poisoning"—at least that's what I told the ER nurses and doctors. Honestly, though, the real reason I went to the emergency room was not because I needed to go. I wasn't in any immediate danger. I went because that's the only way I could stop drinking. The standard protocol for alcohol abuse and dependency was the prescription drug Ativan, which belongs to a class of general sedatives called benzodiazepines. They mimic the effect of alcohol in the brain and are typically administered to offset alcohol withdrawal symptoms and reduce the risk of cardiac arrest. They're also extremely addictive, and the Ativan made it easier to wean myself off the alcohol and get back to some sense of normal. It was the only way to not take one more—*just one more*, I'd tell myself—trip to the store for more booze. But that day was far from normal. I was unemployed for the first time in my life, my general outlook was diminishing by the minute, and looking back, it probably could've gone either way—life or death. I was twenty-eight years old, and this downward spiral had now taken me to rehab and this hospital bed with cheap, thin sheets and cold metal railings.

The incessant beeping is making my head hurt. It makes me want to cry. Cry for help. Cry for lost time. Lost life. But no one can hear me. I'm alone. My left arm is completely black and blue. The nurse missed with the IV. I missed, too, at having a normal life. The swirling contrast of greens and blues and reds seemed to grow by the second, a river of loose blood beneath my skin. Will the bleeding stop? Will the beeping stop? Make it stop. I can't even control that. Can't control anything. My thoughts, my worries. My shame. I've lost control of everything. I'm tired, more tired I've been in my whole life. The alcohol is wearing off. A feeling of total emptiness now. No food, no drink, no spirit, no hope. Only this IV and a terribly bruised arm. A bruised life. I need to pray, but I don't even know what to say. What should I ask for? What do I need? I just need to stop. I know that. But no words come. I have nothing left. And now all I can do is lie here and wait. Wait for something. It's morning, and there's just enough light to keep me going.

I guess I had the wrong idea of what a "dry out" clinic actually was—the meaning of "rehab" or "detox." I envisioned it like a car wash, a place that I could run through quickly and then drive off clean and fresh. Easy, right? Check myself in, get some "medicine," maybe an IV of stuff that would clean me up, and off I'd go. On the contrary, it's anything but a car wash. It's a place of broken souls and new beginnings. It's a place where despair and hope co-exist. And it's a place where people can lose themselves and find themselves all at the same time. I was taken to this place by my decisions alone, or perhaps by my inability to make them—the right ones, anyway. And I was almost taken away from this place, carried off by the angels above. In one way or another, I almost died there.

The doctor arrives. I know the diagnosis. You drink too much. I know the cure. Just don't drink. Pretty simple. The doctor gives me the magic pill. Ativan. *One pill every four hours. Just enough to keep my heart from stopping, but not enough to escape. Only enough to feel half normal, but not enough to forget or to take another time out from life. I crave the numbness more than anything. Anxiety raging. Despair, dread. Still shaking. Six pills. That's it. I checked myself into this place to get clean, and all I got were six little pills. It dawns on me. This isn't going to be easy. The real work is ahead. The rest is on me. I'm starting to do the thing I need to do. Admit defeat. Surrender. The nurse checks my vitals again. All clear. She releases me to the general population. I'm free to roam.*

The only daily requirements at the facility were breakfast, lunch, dinner, and a twelve-step meeting in the chapel room later that night. Needless to say, the next twelve hours felt like twelve weeks. I paced the facility like a crazy person and rarely sat down for more than a couple minutes. I tried to take deep breaths but none would come; I felt out of breath and out of life. But I checked all the boxes. I ate breakfast, lunch, dinner, and sat through a twelve-step meeting with a bunch of people who didn't look like me but resembled me in every way.

As the day went on, and into the night, I felt worse and worse, and it became even harder to breathe. I was very sick and very tired, and I had nothing to take the pain away. Lights-out was at 10:00 p.m., and I slowly made my way to my room through a snaking, dim hallway with flickering fluorescent lights. It resembled an average hospital room, with two laminated wood beds and not much in the way of décor or personality, except for my new bunkmate—another young man about my age. He was on an oxygen ventilator and had tried to commit suicide by locking himself in his garage and breathing the exhaust from his parent's car. He was also addicted to the prescription sleep aid Ambien and had been taking a dozen a day for the past six months. Another gentleman I met that afternoon was a self-proclaimed "career alcoholic," drinking a bottle of vodka a day for the last twenty years. He was shaking so badly he could barely eat his dinner, the rice and peas hopelessly falling from his spoon onto the floor until there were only a couple left to eat.

These two people, looking back, probably scared me straight. Here I was, a weekend binge drinker who let a few sprees get away from him, and by comparison, had entered rehab with his life relatively intact. What I experienced was just the beginning for most addicts, and for me, it could've been a hell of a lot worse, and I was grateful. Even so, I didn't think I could feel much worse. I sat on the edge of that cheap, wood-framed bed and felt a sense of total loss—total destruction. Sleep didn't come easy. The one Ativan pill was like a sick joke, a tease, and certainly not enough to knock me out. In fact, it was just enough for my body to violently crave more. I ached from head to toe, my heart pounded in my chest, and it felt like my soul was being ripped from my body. Perhaps it was. I was in Hell.

It's 2:00 a.m. The nurse is back. Vitals clear. More Ativan. I finally dose off. Awakened suddenly. 3:00 a.m. Not even an hour of sleep. Loud snoring. My new roommate. I sit up with my legs crossed. I'm so tired. My heart aches. My body is heavy. Can't keep my shoulders up. Slumped. Head down. Cheeks in the palms of my hands, where the world used to be. So tired. I'm finished. I cry. I cry hard. I simply can't take it anymore. I'm sick and tired of being sick and tired. I want to scream. I'm ready to surrender. Then I look up. And there it is.

At a most unexpected time, I saw beauty in desolation— the shimmer. Out of nowhere, a dancing rainbow of light started radiating from the upper right corner of my room, just hovering there, watching me. The waves of light rolled and spiraled in place, resonating to the harmony of something higher. It was like nothing I'd ever seen, like a rainbow with personality. It had depth—a tear in the fabric of space, a window to another dimension. It glistened slightly, like it was made of diamonds. It was the most unusual thing I'd ever seen, yet, somehow, I felt it was a part of me. It felt familiar. It felt like love. Pure. Fundamental. Divine. A wave of peace and warmth swept over my body, and I wasn't scared anymore. I wasn't alarmed. It was silent, but it spoke with unspoken words, communicating with me from another world, another realm—a higher dimension. And its message was clear: *I love you. I'm right here. But you're not ready. You're not finished yet.*

I stared at this dancing shimmer of light for several minutes, mesmerized and comforted beyond measure, beyond words. My body no longer ached, the anxiety temporarily relieved. I laid my head down, closed my eyes, and then opened them one last time, looking back to make sure it was still there—and it was. Then, I finally slept. I still wasn't confident that I'd wake up in the morning, but I was at peace. I had all the assurances I ever needed, and I slept better than I had in years.

Day Two

As with most struggles, I didn't learn my lesson the first time. I kept drinking. I stopped for a while, but I picked it back up again a couple months later. And if I thought I felt bad on Day One, I felt really, really bad on Day Two. And after a similar weeklong binge, one with very little eating, and one that ended with an entire bottle of NyQuil because it was too early to buy alcohol that morning, I found myself back in another hospital bed. This time I was in the emergency room of my hometown—the same emergency room I'd been two times before. As they say in twelve-step programs, I was at *"my wits end,"* and with my mother's hand in mine, I admitted for the first time that I'd been defeated. For the first time in my life, I said out loud, "I need help!" And the irony of it all was that I actually didn't need anything. That while I'd become powerless over alcohol, I did have the power. I had the choice. And all I needed to do was to not drink. That was January 20, 2006. A Friday.

To a similar cacophony of blips and beeps, the ER doctor came to see me. The diagnosis was the same, "Son, you drink too much. You might consider not drinking!" So that's what I did. I didn't drink. I never had another drink again. But this time, the doctor gave me fifteen pills, enough for about four days, and discharged me from the ER. I got what I'd come for, and I knew I had one more battle to fight. I returned to my childhood home to begin the countdown and the greatest struggle of my life.

Just like with any addict, the pills didn't last four days. They lasted two and a half. I took my last Ativan on a Monday afternoon, eyeing the bottle all day with a deep and increasing worry—that feeling of impending doom that precedes most panic attacks. Just a couple more hours of painless living ahead of me. And when I went to bed early that night, I didn't sleep much. I tossed and turned, I was hot and cold, each minute an eternity, a hellish grind of cold sweats, heart palpitations, and chest pain. My breathing was erratic, my hands clenched together like vice grips, and my legs shook uncontrollably. I was in bed for the next twenty-four hours.

I thought it was the end. I thought this was the day my heart would finally give out, and I couldn't take it anymore.

At about 7:30 p.m. on Tuesday night, I got up from my bed, put my jacket on, and grabbed my keys. I had to escape the pain, and I was headed out to get another drink. Maybe I could control it this time? *Just one more drink, just so I can sleep tonight, just to make the pain stop.* Maybe I'd magically wake up tomorrow morning and feel better? That's what I told myself, anyway. A few seconds later, my best friend called. He was living in Florida at the time and was just calling to check in. In no uncertain terms, that phone call saved my life. There was also a beautiful woman in my life at the time, and I know I hurt her immensely on Day Two, but I wouldn't be writing this story today if it wasn't for her. She also saved my life. There are no words to thank these two people enough.

After the call—feeling a bit better—I paced around my bedroom for a few minutes and then decided to crawl back into bed, to continue the nightmare of the previous twenty-four hours. By 1:00 a.m., the chest pains and breathing were so bad, I began to fear that I was in a very dire situation. But what could I do? It was the middle of the night, I didn't have the energy to go anywhere, and it seemed like an impossible task to simply get out of bed. I was frozen in time, imprisoned in this ten-by-ten cell in my mother's house. There was no escape, but I had one more choice to make. And with a "twenty-four-hour sober" coin clenched in my right hand—the coin I'd received that previous Saturday morning at a twelve-step meeting—my decision was final, resolute. I was going to live or die in this bed. One of my favorite quotes reminds me of that most critical hour: "Once more into the fray…Into the last good fight I'll ever know. Live and die on this day…Live and die on this day…." And, in a moment of profound confusion and isolation, I saw something more clearly than I had in my life. When all was either lost or gained, there it was again, in the upper right-hand corner of my room—the shimmer—dancing in silence, and speaking the same words as before: *I love you. I'm still here.* This time, I tried to reach out and touch it, but the more I tried to make contact, the more it seemed to fade, as if to remain a mystery, just beyond my mortal grasp.

I lived and I died on that day, an old version gone and a new version yet to be. I never drank again. I picked myself up, and I went to 110 meetings over the next ninety days and never looked back. I never missed it, and I never gave my decision a second thought. That was then, and while I admitted defeat all those years ago, I'm finally the victor. I beat it.

I can't tell you exactly what the shimmer was, but, it was beauty in desolation. It changed something inside me, and it gave me something I desperately needed—a sign—in the form of a dancing rainbow on my two worst days. Maybe it was a hallucination? But somehow, I don't think so. That would stretch coincidence to a most unnatural end—having the exact same experience in such different settings and separated by many months. Perhaps it was the gateway between life and death—the transition between two worlds? I don't know. But if I had to guess, it was probably my soul, temporarily suspended for me to see with my own eyes, that there was still a light left inside me, a light that will always be there. That light has many names. I believe it's called God, it's called the universe, and it's called love. Just like the song from Mumford & Sons, it's our "guiding light."

CHAPTER 5

THE NINETY-YEAR-OLD LITTLE GIRL

*"Your living is determined not so much by what
life brings to you as by the attitude you bring to
life; not so much by what happens to you as by
the way your mind looks at what happens."*

- Khalil Gibran

With my two worst days behind me and about a year of sobriety under my belt, things started to improve. I had my ups and downs, but generally speaking, the trend was going up. Life improved with time, and my daily outlook kept getting better and better. But still single and now in my late twenties, I remember feeling of bit of nagging despair. I had a good job and had recently moved into my first condominium, but I just wasn't going anywhere. I appeared successful and content by most standards, but I hadn't really accomplished anything either. I was still pretty bored, and I just wasn't living…surviving, maybe. But I didn't want to just survive, and as Henry David Thoreau said in *Walden; or, Life in the Woods*, "I wanted to live deep and suck out all the marrow of life, to live so sturdily and Spartan-like as to put to rout all that was not life…" But I was no Spartan, and I knew it.

Not particularly interested in what I was doing profession-ally and certainly a far cry from the physicist I once planned to be, I was idling in my transition to manhood and feeling more alone as each of my childhood friends started to go their separate ways. And for those first several years of sobriety, I was mainly focused on my physical appearance and lifting weights. Not because of the personal records I could tell every-one I was breaking, but mostly due to the latent psychology of a hopelessly undersized and self-conscious kid. Said more simply, I never liked being skinny. The skin and bones only served to manifest a deeper personal discomfort, and I falsely convinced myself that a few extra pounds would make me a happier guy—a true case of body dysmorphia. Perhaps I was trying to be that Spartan on the outside?

Unfortunately, the strength and muscle that was being built on the outside would never compensate for what I lacked on the inside: confidence, a healthy self-image, and a positive attitude. The muscles were just extra layers, ones that would eventually take years to shed. But on a random week-day evening, I saw something that would redefine my concept of strength. Through a small girl with a terrible disease, I was reminded of one of life's most important lessons, that the spirit is far stronger than the body. Her name was Hayley.

Hayley was a little five-year-old girl I saw on a television documentary on one of those lonely nights in the condominium. She had a condition called progeria, which is a genetic disorder that creates an appearance of rapid aging early in a child's life. Most prominent in the facial features, this disease is not particularly merciful. Most people might feel uncomfortable in their presence, and the average lifespan of someone with this disease is thirteen years. It is also extremely rare and, at present, there are just over 160 documented cases worldwide. Needless to say—with those odds—I'd probably feel a bit unlucky, even angry, if this happened to me given the billions of people alive today. But not Hayley!

The documentary highlighted Hayley's first years after being diagnosed as an infant, her countless heart surgeries and long hospital stays, and the highs and lows experienced by her parents and family members. But the program mainly focused on her calm and delicate spirit. It focused on her passion for life, even though she knew it would be cut short. She spoke of Heaven with clarity and excitement, not with vagary and sorrow. The cynics might say: "Well she's young," "She's naïve," "She just believes what her parents tell her to." But I choose to believe that she could see something I couldn't—that the veil is thinnest on the boundaries of our mortality. I choose to believe that whatever her body couldn't provide, her spirit drew from the Divine. And even though her appearance was very different, to me she was beautiful, and I found it impossible to look away.

The image that is forever immortalized in my memory came at the final scene of the documentary, as she eagerly waited for the school bus on her first day of kindergarten. What I'll never forget was how she took take that first step onto the bus, with a smile and a confidence and a pride that I rarely see. I remember how proud I was of someone I'd never know. She's since passed on, but I'll have the chance to speak to her one day, and I'll tell her she's my hero. I'll tell her I admired her attitude, her courage, and her faith and that she would inspire me for the rest of my life. I'll tell her she gave me the winning ticket to a spiritual lottery.

Hayley Okines died on April 2, 2015, at the age of seventeen. In those short years, she became an advocate for the disease and inspired countless people with her courage and determination. She'd appear in numerous other shows and documentaries and would also write two books: *Old Before My Time* and *Young at Heart*.

Isn't it interesting that when I least expected to see God, he showed up in the ninety-year-old face of a five-year-old girl? In an instant, I was given a masterpiece in the timeless art of living, an invaluable portrait from the most unlikely of artists. And the lesson is that attitude is everything. That the difference between happiness and suffering is almost always a choice we can make, a choice to be positive and to give life our best effort regardless of our limitations and how daunting that first giant leap onto the school bus may appear to be.

CHAPTER 6

THE DOWN JACKET

"Don't wait for extraordinary opportunities. Seize common occasions and make them great. Weak men wait for opportunities; strong men make them."

- Orison Swett Marden

I generally think I'm a good person. Most of us probably think the same way of ourselves. But lately, I've been asking an important question: Am I a great person? As much as I aspire to that end, I know I have a lot of work to do. What greatness do I seek, though? There are many forms. Is it the kind that graces the volumes of history or simply the everyday lives of those around me?

Greatness to me is a reflex. It's how we perform in each moment, the displays of love and character without hesitation. It's about doing the right thing without first questioning what the right thing actually is. The opportunities to be great are numbered with the individual moments we have in life, and, needless to say, those are many. That's why I measure greatness this way—because there are countless opportunities in a day to be great. And my scorecard, my evaluation of greatness, is usually binary: Did I succeed or fail? It's usually in my failures where I learn the most, and it's usually in my successes where I find myself closest to God and others. One particular failure changed my life.

I remember a young man with Down syndrome I'd see at the bus stop every morning as I drove to work. He wore a Pizza Hut jacket, and I'd later see him at a location around the corner from my condo, so I knew he worked close by. But then I saw him on that frigid, rainy day in January, completely soaked and miserable. I remember the look on his face and his sense of helplessness. He was vulnerable and alone. Personally, I knew this feeling well. One of the loneliest times in my life was when I couldn't get a ride somewhere after being left behind by someone I was close to.

I remember feeling very sorry for this young man—not necessarily because of his challenges, but because he was standing there alone in the cold with no one to give him a ride to work, which was less than a mile away. But it wasn't because of my empathy that I remember that day. I remember that day because I did nothing. I almost stopped, but I didn't. I hesitated. I hesitated because I felt awkward asking him if he needed a ride. I hesitated because I thought it might be awkward for him, an approach from a total stranger. And the real reason I hesitated, if I'm being completely honest with myself, was because I feared this could become an eventual burden on me. I wasn't mature enough to have a relationship with someone who didn't look like me. That's not something I'm happy to admit.

I'll never know how a simple act of kindness might've affected that young man. Like me, he could've written it down and remembered it for the rest of his life. That day could have led to an unlikely friendship. I just won't know. What I do know is that my greatness was put to the test, and I proved a failure in the moment. But in light of my failure, I vowed to never let that happen again. Little did I know (or perhaps I should've anticipated) my greatness would be tested again, three more times. Three more times over the next eight years, a lot of time to forget the lesson of this first failure.

There's a great scene in the groundbreaking movie *The Matrix* where Morpheus [Laurence Fishburne] is explaining to the protagonist, Neo [Keanu Reeves], about the origins of the computer simulation by the same name—a "computer generated dreamworld" built by an intelligent race of machines to enslave and exploit human beings. Morpheus, upon acknowledging our dependence on machines throughout history, says the following: "Fate, it seems, is not without a sense of irony."

Five years after vowing to "never let that happen again"— leaving someone stranded at a rainy bus stop—I'd arrive at my first of three tests. Leaving the gym one afternoon, I found myself driving through an unexpected downpour, the kind that would soak a person head to toe in seconds. As I slowly crept toward a stoplight on a semi-busy street, I noticed an older gentleman limping along the sidewalk to my right. He was obviously headed to a bus stop several hundred yards ahead and was certainly not going to make it there dry and comfortable. I didn't stop. Again, I did nothing. But about thirty seconds later, as my heart started racing faster and faster—knowing I was abandoning my vow—I slammed on the brakes, turned the car around, and headed back to offer my help. As I pulled up and prepared to roll down my window and ask the old man if he needed help, I witnessed something extraordinary. Someone had beat me to it. A middle-aged man in the car in front of me jumped out in the pouring rain and handed the man an umbrella. And just as quickly as he jumped out to bestow that simple gift, he ran back to his car and drove off. He wasn't expecting his umbrella back or certainly anything in return.

Again, I failed to be great. Not because I didn't make an effort, but because the effort wasn't a reflex. I had to let a subtle, yet compounding sense of guilt send me back to the rescue. And timing is everything. Had I reacted when I should have, that older man would have been dryer and more comfortable on his ride home. Had he gotten the umbrella when he really needed it, history would be different. A mild feeling of shame and disappointment would cling to me for several days.

Three years later, I was headed to the gym on a Wednesday morning before Thanksgiving. It was unseasonably cold, and wind chills were in the low twenties. As I drove along, a young Hispanic woman was walking along the side of the road. Her face and body silently spoke of fatigue and frustration as she struggled with a dozen or so grocery bags. A large aluminum roasting pan fought against the overstuffed bags and a stiff breeze.

This time I didn't hesitate. I stopped my truck, rolled down my passenger window, and asked her if I could give her a ride home. After a couple awkward attempts with loosely coherent Spanish, I was able to get my message across. Reluctant at first, she eventually climbed in, and for the next ten minutes, we didn't say a word. To me, there was a brilliance in the moment that needed no further advance, certainly not from the banality of my half-broken small talk. I dropped her off at her apartment, and with a single tear running down one side of her face, she said, "Thank you," and I simply said, "You're welcome." Worlds apart, worlds collided. Seven minutes later, I'd be tested again.

In an odd twist of fate, after eight years of driving the same route to the gym hundreds of times without seeing him, there he was again—the young man with the Pizza Hut jacket.

The irony was so obvious and so beautiful. The rest I'll leave to your imagination, but this time, I stopped, and through the simple words of a young man with Down syndrome, I heard God say, *Atta boy, Danno. You are a great man today!*

CHAPTER 7

THE STARFISH

"Not everybody can be famous but everybody can be great, because greatness is determined by service."

- Martin Luther King, Jr.

Someone once asked me two important questions: "What is greatness?" and "What is well-doing?" Deep down, I knew the answers, but, unfortunately, it's not how I chose to live my life; not until recently, anyway. For the better part of my life, "great" meant being the best—best looking, best dressed, smartest, funniest, most athletic, most popular, having the best career, the best car, and so on. And my attitude—the one I walked from place to place with—was that I needed to be those things. If I'm being honest, that struggle continues; it may always be there in one form or another.

This was a trap I found myself in for a long time, and it wasn't until someone asked me to define greatness that I started to think and live a bit differently. It forced me to look back on my life and find the opportunities I missed—the people who needed my help and, through my blurry vision of greatness, I failed to serve. How many was it? Ten? One hundred? It was probably too many to count, and I've missed a lot of opportunities to serve because they weren't opportunities to be great, at least not as I defined it. Over time, I've had to re-learn how to be great; and great, like Dr. King said, doesn't mean famous. Great doesn't mean elite. And great doesn't mean better. Great now means something different to me. It means human, simple, ordinary. And the journey to great doesn't end. It's a constant pursuit, and I, like everybody, am always on the way. The world doesn't need more famous people. The world needs more great people.

When asked the question of greatness, I envisioned the somewhat obvious: works of art, successful careers, athletic records, technological discoveries, paradigm shifts, political influence, and military and economic strength. But what really constitutes greatness? Does it have a deeper meaning? Is it accessible to all? I asked myself these questions because I knew my natural default was misguided. Too often in my life, I felt that to be important, to make a difference, I had to accomplish great things, I had to stand above everyone else, I had to do things that others couldn't, and, in a sense, I had to perform miracles. But I finally realized we're all capable of performing miracles, most of the time in very small ways: "Big things have small beginnings," is one of my favorite lines from the 2012 science fiction blockbuster *Prometheus*, which was released shortly after my two children were born. My passion now is to seek greatness in simple things, a thoughtful pursuit of the Divine in the seemingly common—the small beginnings. To me, that's the key. And if we perform small miracles often enough, something great will usually follow. Maybe just start small and see where it goes.

I believe there's no shortage of opportunities to be great: a great father, a great husband, a great friend, a great son, a great coach, a great disciple, a great citizen, a great leader, and most importantly a great human being. The steps we take toward greatness can be small, like composing a personal anthology of modest but powerful moments in time. And being a great human being usually won't make you famous. It doesn't guarantee wealth. Being a great human being isn't a natural reflex, and just like athletics or academics, it takes years of hard work and diligent study.

"Well-doing," then, is the *work* of a great human being: the way we treat each other, raise our children, and teach love rather than hate, courage rather than fear, and respect rather than resentment. It's how we shoulder each other's burdens and embrace each other's successes. It's helping a friend through tough times. It's how we resolve issues with grace and forgiveness. It's showing kindness to a total stranger. It's how we honor the covenants and commandments we have with our creator. It's choosing right when it's so easy to choose wrong. It's how we maintain our character in a world that can quickly distort it. It's acknowledging every day that we have so much to be grateful for. And it's finding joy in the service of others. These are the foundations of greatness, and a great person is tireless in their well-doing.

Just after my wife gave birth to our son and daughter, we received a surprise visit from two acquaintances. I wouldn't even go so far as to call them friends. They knocked on our door, dropped off a small bag with some food, said a few words, and were on their way. It was a nice gesture, but inside the bag was one of the greatest gifts I've ever received, and it would redefine greatness as I previously knew it. It was a short story that would be a turning point in my life. It's called *The Star Thrower* (or "starfish story") by Loren Eisley. It reads:

A young girl was walking along a beach upon which thousands of starfish had been washed up during a terrible storm. When she came to each starfish, she would pick it up, and throw it back into the ocean. People watched her with amusement.

She had been doing this for some time when a man approached her and said, "Little girl, why are you doing this? Look at this beach! You can't save all these starfish. You can't begin to make a difference!"

The girl seemed crushed, suddenly deflated. But after a few moments, she bent down, picked up another starfish, and hurled it as far as she could into the ocean. Then she looked up at the man and replied, "Well, I made a difference for that one!"

The old man looked at the girl inquisitively and thought about what she had done and said. Inspired, he joined the little girl in throwing starfish back into the sea. Soon others joined, and all the starfish were saved.

The message is simple. What if we all picked up a starfish? It's not glamorous. It's not sexy. It won't make the news. It's not a huge burden, nor does it require some unreasonable commitment of our time and energy. But it could make a big difference!

About fifteen years ago, I attended a Bible study with a small church in Northern Virginia. There were a variety of men who attended each week, all from different backgrounds, and each one had unique personalities in one way or another. It was an interesting study, and I met some nice people. But I'll never forget Alex. He was overweight, walked with a cane, and when he spoke—which wasn't often—he spoke softly and with little confidence. He was blind, having lost his eyesight at a young age. He also lost something else—his family. He was abandoned as a child and spent years in the foster care system. Frustration and sadness characterized his every expression, and whatever spirit and light he had left struggled to outshine years of emotional and spiritual darkness. I don't think I ever saw him smile.

I remember how that made me feel. I felt scared for him—deep empathy and sorrow. I felt an overwhelming desire to cure his eyesight, and I wished more than anything that I could heal him. But it wasn't necessarily about him. In a selfish way, I wanted to be the one who returned what he lost, that I'd be known by planet Earth as a miracle worker. Curing his eyesight was only a secondary benefit of my selfish intent. Again, not something I'm proud to admit. And obviously, I couldn't perform that miracle. As it turned out, I didn't perform any miracles at all. Empathy without action, what a shame—what a waste.

I'll never forget Alex, not because I pitied his circumstances or because I felt sorry for him and the emotional impact his situation had on me, but because I should have done more. The great work wouldn't have been to obsess on the supernatural and the title of miracle worker. The great work would have been to be his friend—to talk to him, pray with him, and make sure he knew that somebody cared about him. But that's not what I did. I idled in my desire for greatness. I hesitated. It was easier for me to hope for a miracle rather than to perform a simple act of kindness, which, for him, might have *been* a miracle. What I didn't realize at the time—or perhaps I did—was that I let him down. Maybe I could have made a difference in his life by simply showing him a glimpse of something he may have never known—love. If I met Alex today, I hope things would be different. Maybe he'd be my starfish?

The following article was written by a man named Forest E. Witcraft (1894–1967). He was a scholar, teacher, and Boy Scout executive. The article entitled "Within My Power" was first published in the October 1950 issue of *Scouting Magazine*. You'll probably recognize the final sentence of the article. It's been used in many motivational posters and materials over the years, and I remember it being on the desk of my late Uncle Dave, a great person in my life—a great man. Listen to the words not as they relate to scouting but as how they relate to our responsibility to one another. He writes:

I am not a Very Important Man, as importance is commonly rated. I do not have great wealth, control a big business, or occupy a position of great honor or authority.

Yet I may someday mould destiny. For it is within my power to become the most important man in the world in the life of a boy. And every boy is a potential atom bomb in human history.

A humble citizen like myself might have been the Scoutmaster of a Troop in which an undersized unhappy Austrian lad by the name of Adolph might have found a joyous boyhood, full of the ideals of brotherhood, goodwill, and kindness. And the world would have been different.

A humble citizen like myself might have been the organizer of a Scout Troop in which a Russian boy called Joe might have learned the lessons of democratic cooperation.

These men would never have known that they had averted world tragedy, yet actually they would have been among the most important men who ever lived.

All about me are boys. They are the makers of history, the builders of tomorrow. If I can have some part in guiding them up the trail of Scouting, on to the high road of noble character and constructive citizenship, I may prove to be the most important man in their lives, the most important man in my community.

A hundred years from now it will not matter what my bank account was, the sort of house I lived in, or the kind of car I drove. But the world may be different, because I was important in the life of a boy."[1]

Find your starfish. It could be Alex. It could be your son or daughter, or your mother or father, or a friend, or a neighbor. It could be a total stranger. Or it could be a boy called Joe!

---

1   Used with permission: © *Scouting* magazine / Boy Scouts of America.

CHAPTER 8

THE PIGGYBACK PROPHET

"Any fool can criticize, condemn, and complain—
and most fools do. But it takes character and
self-control to be understanding and forgiving."

- Dale Carnegie, *How to Win*
Friends and Influence People

I n 1936, Simon and Schuster published Dale Carnegie's *How to Win Friends and Influence People*. It'd go on to sell more than thirty million copies worldwide, making it one of the best-selling books of all time. On page seventeen of the 80th Anniversary Edition, he draws his first, and arguably most important, conclusion. He says: "Principle 1: Don't criticize, condemn, or complain."

When I read this passage for the first time, which was shortly after my wife gave birth to our twins, I instantly committed myself to live differently. I've read a lot of things, but there's rarely been a simpler and more powerful instruction, one that I immediately knew I had to follow. In five words, Mr. Carnegie revealed, I believe, two basic secrets to happiness: perspective and gratitude, which is many times a function of perspective. And while the chapter mainly focuses on interpersonal conduct and relationships, particularly in the workplace, it was the last word I found myself most drawn to. "Don't *complain*."

I asked myself: *What do I have to complain about?* And even if there was something, is complaining a wise or mature thing to do? Years later, I'd ask myself if there was another man in the world I'd trade places with, someone else's life I wanted to live other than mine. The answer became clearer in my mind than anything else. The answer was no. I'd be a fool if that answer was different. That answer also became a matter of perspective, and one that would be a source of gratitude and compassion for others going forward.

In preparing a Sunday school lesson for a group of high school students some years ago, I found myself doing some research on world poverty. I uncovered information that I never knew or had even considered—suffering on a scale I didn't know was possible. It led to a shift in my daily paradigm. I generally don't compare myself to other people, but this juxtaposition of the human condition—and the perspective I gained—would be life-changing.

In 2015, according to the World Bank, 734 million people, or 10 percent of the world's population, lived in extreme poverty. This is defined as earning less than $1.90 in equivalent US dollars per day. And while that percentage may seem staggering, it was a dramatic improvement from 1990, when extreme poverty affected 36 percent of the world's population, or 1.9 billion people. In other words, in 1990, just thirty years ago, one in three people on the planet survived on $1.90 or less a day.

To complain, in my personal opinion, is to dishonor the struggles of so many. It's a moral surrender and a foolish compromise of perspective and gratitude. I simply refuse to do it, and over time, I'd learn to silence a continuous but subtle murmuring that plagued my pursuit of happiness—my pursuit of peace. And one particular photograph changed everything. During my research, I came across a picture of a skinny, malnourished African child giving his younger brother a piggyback ride through garbage and mud. We've all seen it. Both were extremely frail and obviously very sick, in tattered clothes and barefoot. The older brother's tiny feet were dwarfed by large tread tracks neatly imprinted in the rain-soaked mud, the tracks of a vehicle none of us want in our front yard—a vehicle of war. But his eyes were ignited in spirit; they blazed with strength and resolve.

I wondered what was really going on in that scene. Was the elder protecting his brother from the harsh environment? Was the younger brother disabled or injured and unable to walk? Or maybe—just maybe—despite extreme and obvious hardship, they were just trying to have a little fun. Whatever it was, it was an absolute triumph of the human spirit.

Our prophets and teachers are everywhere, and they often reveal themselves in simple, unexpected, and mysterious ways—the way the Lord, I believe, has intended it. It's our responsibility to open our eyes to the beauty around us and to listen to what it has to say. But that's always a choice we have to make. We can choose to be dissatisfied with our lives and what we've gone without, or we can dive deeply within ourselves and progress toward an eternal goal, which is the ultimate advancement of our being. We do that through love, compassion, and gratitude. The examples are out there if we know where to look, and it's worth repeating: They're everywhere!

That fervent reminder from the Piggyback Prophet, in retrospect, was a timely coincidence to a totally random personal revelation I had in my closet (of all places) a couple months before. Rooting around trying to find some gym clothes and lamenting on some inane problem I had at the time, I realized that I was actually choosing to be unhappy. It was easier to feel sorry for myself than to not, and so I did, and I did it often. In that moment in my closet, I made a commitment to recognizing the thoughts and behaviors that propagated such a paltry and wasteful utilization of my time and energy. It's not a difficult exercise. In fact, it's quite easy. The difficult part is to suppress or otherwise ignore self-destructive thoughts. I'm happy to say that those thoughts and behaviors have rarely seen the light of day since. But it requires constant monitoring. It requires, like anything, a diligent and honest effort, because it's easy to complain, feel sorry for yourself, and to be dissatisfied. These are completely passive behaviors, and they come to us by default if we're not careful.

In light of my revelation, though, I still had to ask myself some honest questions. How many beautiful things had I missed? How many experiences had I lost in my obsession with being dissatisfied? Did dwelling on the negative affect my ability to see the subtle beauties and miracles in my life? Did my lack of perspective for the suffering of others numb an already troubled heart? I was saddened by my answers: a lot, yes, and yes. It was important to recognize these losses, but not to dwell on them. I asked these questions only once, and then I decided to move on, and every day following that night in the closet has been different, more joyful, and closer to God. For most of us, maybe it's possible to be happy by simply choosing not to be unhappy.

The Piggyback Prophet would also become a brilliant example of an under-appreciated truth in life—that sometimes we don't get what we ask for. In fact, many times it's just the opposite. We pray for happiness, for relief, for peace, for wealth, for a way out, and for health. We pray for answers and for help in difficult situations. We pray for miracles. But more often than not, we don't receive direct answers; certainly not the ones we immediately want, anyway. Miracles seem few and far between. I think of that little boy often. I also think of the billions of prayers that children like him have asked. I wonder if some of mine seem silly by comparison.

Many years after my encounter with the Piggyback Prophet, I'd re-read the gospel account of Jesus's final days in a much different light. It would fundamentally change my basic expectations in life and how I'd approach prayer in general. Shortly before he was betrayed, arrested, and crucified, Jesus took refuge in a small garden called Gethsemane on the Mount of Olives in Jerusalem. Knowing the imminent pain and suffering he'd endure, he said to his disciples: *"My soul is overwhelmed with sorrow to the point of death."* (Matthew 26:38) The next verse goes on to say: "Going a little farther, he fell with his face to the ground and prayed, *'My Father, if it is possible, may this cup be taken from me.'"*

I'll never read that passage the same way again. Despite his power, Jesus was afraid. He was uncertain of his future, and he asked his father to deliver him from the torment that lay just ahead and from his responsibility as savior—in fact, he'd ask two more times. In plain words, Jesus says, "Father, I can't do it. Please help me." He's undeniably human in the moment—

just like us—and that's why I love him. He took on a human form to say, "I understand what you're going through. I'll do it myself, and to show you how much I love you, I'll walk the line as well."

I asked myself a few life-changing questions: *Was his prayer answered? Was it answered in the way he wanted? Was his responsibility lifted? Did his life get any easier?* The answer to all of these questions is no, and his life would get a hell of a lot harder from that point forward.

Minutes after that prayer in the Garden, Jesus would be betrayed by someone close to him, then arrested, humiliated, beaten, and tortured to within an inch of his life. In the end, he was nailed to a cross and left to die. He endured a level of pain and suffering I can't even imagine. But in the process, he'd inspire billions. He'd conquer death, he'd give us an example of how to really live, and his words would echo across eternity. His unanswered prayer changed history, and it changed me.

If Jesus's prayers weren't answered that night in the Garden, if his father didn't do that for his own son, then maybe I needed to re-evaluate my prayers—those that often serve the selfish and materialistic needs of my first-world experience. Maybe I needed to understand something more basic—that life is supposed to be difficult, that to a large extent, we're on our own, and that there's no glory in being handed something simply because I asked for it. Maybe I should expect to earn everything and be handed nothing. Maybe happiness itself is earned.

It's pretty simple. I need to have faith. I need to put my head down, and with that same fire and resolve—like the boy in that photograph—live the best life I can. Life's not fair for a lot of us. We often don't choose the conditions or situations that we find ourselves in, but we can choose how we respond. We can change our experience, which then changes history, both backward and forward. But we first need to remember rule number one: "Don't complain!" Instead, pick something up, whether it's a brother in need or your own cross.

CHAPTER 9

THE YELLOW FLICKER OF HOPE

"If you can fill the unforgiving minute
With sixty seconds' worth of distance run,
Yours is the Earth and everything that's in it,
And—which is more—you'll be a Man, my son!"

- If, Rudyard Kipling

S hortly before my beautiful and tougher-than-nails wife gave birth to our twins, Chase and Berkeley, we moved to a small neighborhood in a calm suburb of Northern Virginia—just a short walk from my in-laws. It was a wonderful time in our lives, filled with love and support from friends and family. But as you can imagine, as first-time parents of twins, we were tired all the time. Every day was the same as every other, and I could rarely, with any discernible intelligence or logic, remember what I had done two days ago. It was a blurry time in my life but one of the most clear and vivid at the same time.

It was a deeply spiritual experience. I seemed to survive on that energy alone, and if you've ever doubted the existence of angels, or another dimension of reality, just peer into the eyes of an infant—the pure wonder they express when experiencing the world for the first time. And perhaps they see something we don't, something we've long forgotten. Perhaps, just for an instant, the curtains are still drawn, letting the light and mysteries of the universe shine through.

But despite the spiritual adrenaline I seemed to be surviving on, I was still pretty tired. The only activity I had was a few runs here and there, and even those seemed blurred and unremarkable. But on one random afternoon, on a short jog like any other, I saw the greatest runner I'd ever seen, someone I'll always remember with total clarity. He was a young boy in a fluorescent yellow T-shirt, and the most graceful runner I'd seen or would ever see. I saw him often after that first time. In my mind, I coined him "The Yellow Flicker of Hope," a nuclear power plant of sheer will. He had obvious physical limitations and appeared to run almost sideways from a strong limp and a badly hunched back. His face and head were somewhat contorted and pitched forward as if he struggled to see from just one eye. But he ran faster than I did!

I remember how tired I was on those runs. I remember how out of shape I felt and how much I didn't feel like running. But without speaking a word and through his marvelous stride, the young boy told me this: *Don't ever complain. Don't ever say you're too tired. Don't ever say your legs hurt. Don't ever say it's too hard or I can't. And never, ever feel sorry for yourself.* He's a compelling witness to one of my favorite quotes by speaker and running writer John Bingham. He said,

"What distinguishes those of us at the starting line from those of us on the couch is that we learn through running to take what the day gives us, what our body will allow us, and what our will can tolerate."

I remember the one time the boy and I crossed paths, almost close enough to reach out and touch one another. I remember the bolts of lightning that struck my heart and the energy that radiated through my soul. With adrenaline seething through my veins, I turned around, trotted backward for just a minute, and watched a master at work. I let out a silent roar and, with a clenched fist, pumped my right arm to what was one of the greatest events of my life—a silent tribute to one of the greatest humans who's ever lived.

It was a powerful reminder of exactly how strong we really are, regardless of how tired and imperfect our bodies may be. It was a reminder that will is an essential element of the universe and simply no match for the difficulties we all face in life. It's no coincidence that some of my best runs have been when I was the most tired and the most reluctant to get up and go—ones where I had to rely on will alone.

I'm not a particularly fast runner, but I'd never run the same way again. From that point forward, I'd run from the heart, like a blazing fire—it found a home inside me. I'd rarely concede to pain or discomfort; and in his eternal memory, I'd learn to disregard weakness—in most of its forms—and to accomplish whatever goal I had that day. He taught me that the current mile is the only one that matters, not the first or the last; and looking back, I have to ask myself: *Who was more disabled?* He ran faster, overcame more, his will far exceeded mine, and, most importantly, he inspired me beyond measure. I hope we meet one day. If we do, I'll tell him I saw God in his stride. I'll tell him I felt redeemed by the rhythmic beauty of his unique cadence. I'll tell him to keep running, because the longer he runs, the more hearts he'll touch, just like he touched mine.

Eight years after that first encounter—after we'd had moved to a new neighborhood a short distance away—I saw him again, now a man. On a random summer afternoon, as I pulled up to a stop sign just outside my in-laws' neighborhood, there he was again in that yellow shirt, now slightly faded and pulled at the ends, but every bit as bright. This time, he paused and looked right at me. His message was clear. *I haven't slowed down. I haven't given up. What about you?*

A couple months later, I was driving to a family get together with my son Chase—now eight years old. This time it was dark, but the headlights of my F-150 caught a familiar yellow flicker in the distance, and his graceful stride struck my retinas once again. I'd go on to tell Chase about this runner. I told him that I wrote a story about him and how his example changed my life. Then, my son said something incredible, and it's difficult for me to repeat without getting very emotional. He said, "Well, Daddy, maybe you'll get a chance one day to tell him you wrote a story about him." Maybe I will.

If I do, I'll tell him about the name I gave him: the Yellow Flicker of Hope—a warrior, a champion, a role model, a leader, the greatest runner the world has ever known, and a great man. I'll tell him the world needs more men like him and that he fills the unforgiving minute far greater than I do. But above all, I'll tell him he's my hero, and I'll tell him I love him.

In life, sometimes we're tired. Sometimes we feel inadequate. And sometimes we think that all is lost. But keep your eyes open, because maybe one winter day, you'll see a yellow flicker in the distance. A glimmer of hope that will bring you more love and strength than you ever thought possible. That yellow flicker might just change your life.

CHAPTER 10

THE AMBASSADOR

"Example is not the main thing in influencing others. It is the only thing."

- Albert Schweitzer

On a day like any other—recently—I was out running and a song came on my playlist. It was my favorite rendition of "Amazing Grace" by the American folk singer Judy Collins. I admit that "Amazing Grace" is an odd choice for a workout mix, but honestly, it's for moments like this. I was running along and was completely stunned by the final verse. I've heard it many times before, but on that beautiful summer afternoon, I heard it differently.

When we've been there ten thousand years,
Bright shining as the sun,
We've no less days to sing God's praise,
Than when we first begun.

As the tears ran down my face, I experienced an odd flash-back of the last ten thousand years of human history. I was inspired by the beautiful things we've accomplished as a spe-cies—the progress we've made, the masterpieces we've created, and the love we've shown each other. I was also overwhelmed by our cruelty—the evil that exists in the world, the broken dreams, and the shattered lives. In that simple moment, I found a deep musing of my faith, and I've come to person-ally understand the balance of good and evil and why oppo-sition is necessary in life. But I've yet to discover why we fall so short of that simple commandment Jesus gave us—to *love one another, as I have loved you.*"

This experience came full circle about a week later when I finished a wonderful little book by Og Mandino called *The Greatest Salesman in the World.* The title's a little misleading, but one of the chapters challenged me to rise every morn-ing and greet each day with love in my heart. What a sim-ple charge. What a simple commission. I can only imagine that those ten thousand years would've been different if we all did the same.

Now for whatever reason, this experience reminded me of a random encounter I'd had with someone twenty years earlier and over four thousand miles away. His name was Marcel. Marcel was a PhD student from Kenya whom I met on a train from Innsbruck, Austria to Rome, Italy. He was studying in Vatican City and preparing for his dissertation in theology. He was soft-spoken and a true gentleman. I'd just graduated from college and was on a backpacking trip through Europe with two childhood friends. That night, we shared an overnight compartment with Marcel for the eight-hour trip to Rome.

It was an odd foursome—three rowdy white boys and one super educated black man from a world away. But something clicked. A strange bond formed that would transcend economics, politics, religion, culture, or any of our other inherent differences. I remember how we laughed together and how much I admired his humble and quiet demeanor. He had a very calming presence, and his perspectives on life were truly refreshing and stood in stark contrast to my experience as a suburban, upper middle-class American. I savored every moment. The next day, Marcel would become an ambassador for the ages.

When we arrived at the train station in Rome, Marcel said only two words, two words that reminded me of the graceful reverence and meekness Jesus displayed as he gathered his disciples along the Sea of Galilee: "Follow me." How could I not remember him as a momentary incarnation of my Lord and Savior? We the sheep and he the shepherd. Marcel then led us on a VIP tour of Rome, showing us places we would have never seen on our own. It was an act of grace and charity that was unmatched by any in my lifetime. Eventually, he showed us to our hotel, and we said our goodbyes. It was a bittersweet moment as I knew I'd probably never see him again. But we saw each other again ten minutes later, and that reunion, combined with a fifteen second conversation, would change me forever. In those fifteen seconds, he humbly uttered a phrase that should be repeated across the universe—and across eternity.

After Marcel left, my friends and I spent a few minutes chatting about the day and then checked in to our hotel. I looked down to pick up my pack and there it was, Marcel's briefcase. I panicked and, without hesitating, I took off running. I knew that finding Marcel would be unlikely, given it was rush hour in one of the largest cities in Europe.

In a dead sprint through the torrid afternoon heat of Rome, I finally found him. I presented him the briefcase and, to my surprise, he only returned a curious grin. Did he know I'd be the one to return what he left behind? That maybe in an odd converging of destinies, his mistake was purposeful. What transpired next would be one of the most powerful events of my life. It was something he said to me, his parting request. It brings tears to my eyes every time I think of it and many years later—on that run—I'd know the next ten thousand years could be different if we were all a little more like him, if we'd follow his example. I'd never see Marcel again, but he'll be a friend for life, my eternal travel companion and a constant reminder of the selfless gifts we can give.

Now, standing together again, it dawned on me that I never properly thanked him for what he did for us. I politely asked him to join us for dinner. He declined and I said, "But Marcel, how can we ever repay you? You've been so good to us and so generous with your time." With his kind and soft voice, he said this: "Don't worry about it, my friend, but when I come to your country, you do the same for me."

CHAPTER 11

THE PEARL

"I am nothing special, of this I am sure. I am a common man with common thoughts and I've led a common life. There are no monuments dedicated to me and my name will soon be forgotten, but I've loved another with all my heart and soul, and to me, this has always been enough."

- Nicholas Sparks, The Notebook

"What's your favorite parable in the New Testament?" someone once asked me. Without hesitating I said, "The Parable of the Pearl of Great Price." Matthew 13: 45–46 says this: "Again, the kingdom of heaven is like a merchant in search of fine pearls. When he found one very precious pearl, he went away and sold all he had and bought it."

The traditional interpretation of this parable is that we are the merchant man. We spend a lifetime seeking things that are beautiful, things that give us meaning and hope, as well as things that bring us comfort and happiness. Eventually, though, we find one thing in particular, the one thing we would give up everything to have. A pearl in this case. The pearl is meant to represent the kingdom of Heaven and to illustrate the great value of everlasting life and the path home to God.

Some time ago, I came across a lesser-known interpretation of this parable, and it made a lot of sense. Perhaps the kingdom of Heaven and Jesus Christ are the merchant man, and *we're* the pearl. After all, the parable does say the kingdom of Heaven is like the merchant man. It doesn't say that we are like the merchant man. Accordingly, I believe that God endlessly searches for us, and Jesus gave up everything he had so that we would live. It makes more sense that the kingdom of Heaven is not something that can be bought. It's a gift, from someone who loves us more than we'll ever know on this Earth, from some place where we won't need eyes to see.

This parable confirms the only certainty I have in life. And if I'm being truly honest with myself, how many certainties do I really have? I believe in the general goodness of people. I believe in our democracy and the American ideal. I believe in my talents and my character, and I believe in the gospel of Jesus Christ. But people will always let us down. All nations will eventually crumble. I'll fail many times throughout my life, and my character will be challenged often. I didn't witness the resurrection.

I have a strong belief in many things, but there's only one thing I'm absolutely certain of and that's the love I have for my children. They're my pearls of great price, my greatest treasure. And just like the merchant man and Jesus Christ, I would give up my life for them. The experience of being a parent—the pure love of a child—is not one that is adequately described by words, and I'm grateful for the experience of being a father, because for the first time in my life I understood God's love. I finally understood exactly how much my creator loved me when I, too, became a creator. This love between parent and child reminds me of a beautiful passage from a book I recently read called *The Journey Home* by Radhanath Swami. It reads:

> The day before I was to leave home for college, my father was especially emotional. "Richie," he said, "let's take a ride together." We drove along the tranquil streets of Highland Park's Sherwood Forest, surrounded by the sounds of children laughing and playing. "Son," he began, "as long as I'm alive, I'm always here for you." Stopping the car, he held my hand as his voice quivered, "As your father, I expect you to do your best, but whether you succeed or fail, do good or bad deeds, or even betray me, as long as I'm alive, I'll love you and I'm here for you. This is a promise I will live and die to keep. Please, never forget this.[2]

---

2 Radhanath Swami, *The Journey Home* (CA: Insight Editions, 2010).

It was a timeless analogue to the love I have for my own children, and I'd repeat those words to them that same night. I repeat them as often as possible. Why is "The Pearl of Great Price" my favorite parable? Because it confirms for me that love is the only universal truth, and it's the foundation of all things. It's the one and only thing I'll ever truly know—it may be the only knowledge I actually need.

In its purest form, love is not complicated. It's something we all understand. It's tangible and real, and it's the fifth dimension. It's where God resides. It's his home, a place just beyond our capability to see, but certainly something we can feel. Love is the only thing that matters.

One of my favorite movies is *Interstellar* by Christopher Nolan. The plot centers on a group of astronauts traversing a black hole to find a new home for mankind. The main character, played by Matthew McConaughey, makes a decision early in the movie to leave his young son and daughter, knowing that he'll not return for many years. He makes this sacrifice to save humanity from an impending disaster, and, as you can imagine, it's a hard thing to watch as a parent. Later in the movie, the crew finds themselves in a tense and highly fraught race against time.

The movie also does a good job of explaining a natural phenomenon called time dilation. It's the center construct of Einstein's theory of general relativity, and it proves that speed and gravity influence time itself, that time is not constant everywhere in the universe. It's fluid, and changes based on an object's movement through space relative to another. The faster you go or the stronger the gravity, the slower time passes for you and the faster time passes for everyone else.

So, in the movie, the characters find themselves in between these strong gravity environments where minutes for them are the equivalent to years back on Earth. As the mission begins to unravel, Matthew McConaughey's character starts to realize that due to this warping of time, he's not going to make it home to see his son and daughter—certainly not as he remembered them. Obviously, this is a difficult situation, and his co-star Anne Hathaway tries to comfort him. She says: "Love isn't something that we invented. It's observable. Powerful. It has to mean something. Maybe it means something more, something we can't yet understand. Maybe it's some evidence, some artifact of a higher dimension that we can't consciously perceive. Love is the one thing that we're capable of perceiving that transcends dimensions of time and space."

Our physical universe—time itself—can be twisted, bent, squeezed, and stretched, but love is the only true universal constant. Love can't be broken, and I believe that no matter how far away or separate we feel from God or a loved one, whether it's across the universe or in a distant dream or prayer, it's love that connects us. It's love that will bring us together one day. Love will bring us home.

Another of my favorite quotes is from Victor Hugo's *Les Miserables* where he asks: "What is Love? I have met in the streets a very poor young man who was in love. His hat was old, his coat worn, the water passed through his shoes and the stars through his soul." Very simply, love is the only thing that matters, and this quote reminds me of several experiences I had a couple of years back.

I was at a gas station picking up something to drink when an older woman walked in. It was immediately clear she was experiencing homelessness. Her clothes were filthy, and she smelled terrible. She was shaking and obviously very sick. When she got to the register, she pulled out a handful of loose change and bought a lottery ticket. But all these things were secondary to the look I saw in her eyes. There was a total absence of life, an absence of hope. Her eyes were blank, fearful, and confused, and they told a very sad story.

This woman didn't need to win the lottery. She didn't need a shower or a fresh set of clothes. She didn't need a job or a roof over her head. More than anything, she needed to know that someone loved her, that she had a divine purpose, and the struggles she faced in mortal life would one day be redeemed. I'm not sure how I could've helped that woman in the gas station, and every day we see countless brothers and sisters that we'll never reach and who will continue to struggle. But I believe one day, it'll all make sense. I believe love will win.

A couple of weeks later, I was out on a run and passed a small Asian girl on the sidewalk. She couldn't have been more than nine or ten years old. What initially stood out was that she was alone. I didn't see anyone with her or anyone else close by. Her body was terribly crippled, and it was obviously difficult for her to walk. But what stood out most was the way she was dressed. Her outfit was as cute as could be, perfectly coordinated and brand new. The clothes were so sharp and vibrant that they actually drew attention to her disability. But that didn't seem to matter to her, and it certainly didn't matter to me. She wasn't ashamed, and she had done her best to look pretty that day. Don't we often hide our imperfections and vulnerabilities from the world? I gave her the warmest smile I could, as if to silently say, *I'm proud of you and I love you*, because that's all that mattered.

I find great inspiration in those who overcome disability and misfortune, because I'm not sure I could. Matthew 25 speaks of the "least of these my brethren." We've all heard it. Most of us probably think it means to help those who can't help themselves, to serve those with disabilities and hardship. But I've come to learn that more often "the least of these" is me—that those who overcome significant challenges are stronger than I'll ever be. They have a love in their heart far greater than mine, and they provide me with things I many times don't have: resilience, inspiration, courage, faith, and determination.

Lastly, I'd like to tell you about a little prayer my daughter Berkeley—my princess—said one evening a couple years ago. On September 10, 2017, the eye of Hurricane Irma made landfall a couple miles from my parents' home in Marco Island, Florida. Tidal surges were estimated at ten to fifteen feet, and even at ten feet, the island would've been completely destroyed. Berkeley came to me the night before and said, "Daddy I'd like to say a prayer for NaNa and Grandad." I think she could tell I was concerned for my parents, the imminent destruction of their home, and the heartache of having to start over, especially at a later stage in life. What followed was one of the most sincere and loving things I've ever heard, something I'll never forget. It was a soft and delicate plea to keep her grandparents safe, and that she loved them very much.

In the end, the island was spared. Storm surges never reached above seven feet. Now, did her prayer push back that massive storm? I don't believe so. To do so would be to embrace a most unreasonable comparison. Billions of similar prayers have been prayed without that kind of result. Was her prayer better? Did God listen to her over another? Was she a better person and therefore God was more willing to help? Those questions are unanswerable, and any attempts to answer them would presume God's agenda, which I won't do. But her prayer reminded me, and will continue to remind me, of a simple lesson—little things can sometimes make a big difference. And that most things in life are no match for the love in a six-year-old's heart.

If there's anything in your heart that doesn't belong there, if you have feelings, thoughts, resentments, dissatisfaction, pain, or anything that wouldn't be right in the eyes of God, or if there's suffering, anxiety, worry, or depression, if you can, let it go. Find the love in all things, and find the things that carry its message. It can be a passage from scripture, a movie, a book, a homeless woman in a gas station, a disabled girl in your neighborhood, or the prayer of a six-year-old little girl. Their message is timeless: there's enough love for all of us. Love is everywhere, and it's the only thing that really matters.

CHAPTER 12

THE YIN
(THE DARKNESS)

*"I don't believe in the Devil. You don't need
him, people are bad enough by themselves."*

- Devil, M. Night Shyamalan

I t's a question that's been asked forever, and it's a great question. But it's also a tough question, perhaps the toughest of all? Maybe it's a question that's beyond human understanding—something we're not supposed to know for sure but only ponder. It's a question that the non-religious use to deny a benevolence in the universe, and a question that believers lament in their darkest hours. It's a question—and a somewhat obvious, but hidden answer—that may just provide proof of a loving God, that love is the most important thing of all, and that freedom and mortality are the greatest gifts we've been given. It's a question that in over four decades on this Earth—and despite the thousands of pages I've read on the subject—I didn't find a good answer to, until one random evening in a place I never expected. It's a question that's plagued the human condition since the beginning, a question that an ordinary guy like me may have finally answered—at least in his own life. *Why does evil exist?*

The yoga studio at Lifetime Fitness in my hometown in Northern Virginia is a sanctuary, an oasis. It's one of the most comfortable places I've ever been. It's dimly lit, warm, inviting, and there's an energy within its walls that's manifest. There's an immediate sense of peace, love, and gratitude, as if the people inside know it's a special place, and they act accordingly—deferring the respect it has earned. When I enter the studio, I'm always welcomed by a soft breeze and a delicate harmony of scents and sounds, each one gracing every nerve ending of my body. The music alone is enough to calm my worries, even for the short time I spend there. As I said, it's a sanctuary—a safe place.

Before class, people of all kinds congregate in a small waiting area to remove their shoes and place them in a neat bank of cubbies along one wall. On another wall is a painting, something basic, yet so colorful and strong. It's subtle and inviting, yet complex, with symbols and imagery from spiritual traditions I yearn deeply for, things I want to know more about, and places that I believe hold secrets I need to discover. The prana, or energy, is electric, like my hair could stand on end, and a series of potted flowers and plants bring me into a presence with nature, and into my divine nature. I feel at home, like my soul has arrived at a place it wants to be. It's a beautiful place, and it's about to bestow one of the most beautiful gifts I've ever received.

The studio is perched on the second floor of the facility and is surrounded on two of its four sides with floor-to-ceiling windows. Long, earth-colored drapes fall from the ceiling to a hidden line of string lights, encasing the room in a faint, but comforting orange glow. The drapes provide a kind of barrier from the noise and chaos that lay just outside, the hectic and sometimes confusing shuffle of the outside world, and of my mind. The practice itself is a form of yoga called Yin. It's a series of seated postures that participants hold for three to five minutes, stretching the fascia and muscles. It's a deeply meditative experience, and the average class is about an hour. For that hour, my eyes are closed, but on one ordinary, spring evening just a short time ago, I opened them. The drape on the far wall had been temporarily pulled aside—a crack in the ether—exposing a setting sun on the horizon and a vivid, but hidden truth.

What I saw—the silhouette in that window—would change my view of the world, forever. But it wasn't anything supernatural. It wasn't extraordinary. It's probably something that's happened a thousand times without anyone giving much notice. It was an ordinary event; basic, fundamental, but it was magnificent. It was a simple human interaction, and one of the most beautiful things I've ever seen.

The silhouette, overlaid on that setting sun and a backdrop of tall trees, sharply outlined the instructor kneeling behind one of the participants, who was positioned on their side facing the tall window, and despite the dark and greyish blur to it all, the image was beautiful—almost divine. The instructor's slender arms and hands were outstretched like an angel, descending slowly with pure love and intention, and resting gently on the participant's shoulder and torso—a deliberate and beautiful nexus of skin and soul. Her head and blond ponytail were bowed slightly, perhaps into a thoughtful prayer, submitting herself to another in total love and devotion.

It was one of the most present and selfless acts of grace and beauty I'd ever seen, one person in complete service of another and two people unified in the serenity of this awesome place. In its simplicity—the humble and loving service of one human being for another—it changed something inside me. I'd never observe basic human interactions the same way again. I'd begin to see them as anything but ordinary, the product of the Divine, a typically unnoticed remnant of our eternal ancestry. But it drew an important contrast, an important question. How could what I just saw coexist with such hardship—such evil—and most importantly, why? Where does the darkness come from?

We live in a place where, for lack of a better phrase, a lot of bad shit happens, which I admit, is the ultimate rhetorical understatement, and I'm not naïve enough to think that it won't continue. I'm a firm believer in competition and its natural results: winners and losers. However, we seem to lose a lot—a lot of loss occurs. Unfortunately, it seems to be the nature of the world, and yet, why? Why does there continue to be such hardship, such evil?

We wage unnecessary wars, we let children starve, we fill our brains and hearts with bad information, we wear wrist watches that well exceed in cost what most people on the planet make in a lifetime, we persecute and exploit the weak and underprivileged. At the same time, we pretend like we actually care about others, that 99 percent of our focus and attention isn't given to our own self-interest—apathy being the real and unacknowledged epidemic. Most of us say we should help the poor, but how often do we actually have them over for dinner? How often do we lift a finger to change the nature of the world? This book, and hopefully many more like it, is my attempt to do just that.

I said in the introduction that I wouldn't cast judgment, but in this case, I just can't help myself. For centuries, people have been trying to rationalize and tell us why bad shit happens. The predominant philosophy, or rather theology, is that some hidden, demonic force drives us to do bad things, that we're at the unwitting influence and control of this scary guy called the devil, that it's not our fault—a foolish cop-out that's held us unchecked and unaccountable for thousands of years. But that's not all bad news, there's a solution, and churches and mostly old, white men have been telling us how to avoid him, how to stay out of Hell.

In my opinion, Hell is a ridiculous place. It's not the origin of evil nor is it the place we go when we've been naughty—failing to live up to the expectations of God. We don't go there by default, because we're inherently imperfect, or because we've been the unlucky inheritors of sin, hinged to the decisions of two people in a mystical garden a very long time ago. We don't have to claw our way out of the inferno, through some comical and self-righteous odyssey to perfection—in search of the unattainable Golden Fleece. In fact, a perfect world with perfect people in it—a world also with no death or challenge—doesn't even make sense.

There would be no forward progress in a perfect world, so to say that perfection was the original utopia—the original intent—and that somehow, we screwed things up is an oversimplified and under-analyzed conjecture at best. The Garden of Eden—as an allegory—actually promotes the idea of individual choice, that each choice we make has a consequence, every action a reaction. Unfortunately, the choices made in the story of the Garden of Eden have been used against us, to say that we're forever imperfect in the eyes of God, that we're continuously tempted by the devil, and that sin and death were not in the original plan, that they exist in our world only because of us—our mistakes. I disagree. The fall of man was inevitable. It was planned. God knew it was going to happen. Period. The end.

Imagine playing a video game that has no challenges, no danger, no fear, no monsters lurking around every corner, no mystery; a game that you can win every time with little effort. That would get boring pretty quickly, and it would lack purpose. A perfect world sets up an infinite regression the opposite way, toward higher and higher levels of perfection, toward a Heaven that has a scorecard, or toward someone saying that we're not there yet, but keep trying, keep praying, keep paying—then maybe you'll get there. And if you don't get there, you're to blame, you did something wrong. And by the way, if you don't get there my way, then it doesn't count. You're not saved and tough shit—to Hell you go. For a multitude of reasons, the paradox that is Hell can't exist. It's illogical, short-sighted, and inherently purposeless, with no historical or rational precedent.

Very simply, I believe, Hell is a place we invented for our own selfish reasons, to control and manipulate people, to create an artificial and desperate need for hope—or relief, to sooth the fear of death and annihilation. Hell created a self-perpetuated dependence on powerful people, a perennial cash flow for the keepers of the gate keys, the proverbial self-licking ice cream cone for history's elite. Do what I say and I'll keep you safe from that horrible place. And not only will you not suffer, but you'll also live forever! You'll never die, the thing you fear most!

This system set up a lazy and nebulous shortcut to an already discernible reality. My simple recommendation is to just read a few books—in my case physics, Christian, eastern tradition, Buddhist, Hindu, philosophy, psychology, mathematics, New Age, and spiritual—and you'll come to the same, rather obvious conclusion…that there's probably a lot more going on behind the scenes than we know, and we'll likely be okay in the end, if there even is one. Time, as Albert Einstein once said is *"only a stubbornly persistent illusion."* That the fantastic and utterly mind-blowing complexity of the universe didn't just happen, that it has some purpose, and it's purpose is love, but not to condemn. You'll also conclude that there's been a systematic and irresponsible distortion of the original messages of Earth's greatest prophets, that you need to read between the lines created by the parochial and deliberate telephone game we've played across history—the greatest apostasy of human truth. Perhaps The DaVinci Code was onto something after all, *"so dark the con of man."* In our grand wisdom, we traded prophets for profiteers and fact for fiction.

From everything I've read, which is way more than the old white men would like, I almost guarantee that death is not what we think it is. There's no such thing. There's nothing to fear. Fear, as history continues to prove, is a well-understood and abused motivator, maybe third in line to love and ultimately, to survival itself—eating, breathing, sex.

Even as a child, I couldn't rationalize the existence of Hell. I couldn't place it in the context of a loving God. In fact, in Genesis in the Old Testament, one statement always stood above the rest—that we're created in his image. It never seemed reasonable, especially now as a parent, that God would send his children to a place of eternal suffering—the fiery pit—because we screwed up, because we didn't honor and respect his rules. I just simply can't reconcile Hell with a loving God, with my eternal parent. It's not in his image or in the image of love. It's in the image of the worst in all of us, mere mortals.

I'll never condemn my children—not ever—and I doubt you would either. Hell and the devil are not only deeply conspired constructs of our own making, they're disappointing surrenders of basic intelligence, reason, and human love. In fact, if Heaven is a place that draws the distinction between a megalomaniacal God, one who allows the torture of his own children, and every ordinary parent I know—those who have the complete and unconditional love and support for their children and who would do anything for them—I don't want to go. It's not a place I want to be and it's not the company I want to keep.

There's been a conscious and unified effort to separate people for centuries—those who are going to Hell and those who aren't—and yet we wonder why there's such division, such hatred. No thank you! I'll take my chances! Native American activist and theologian Vine Deloria, Jr. perhaps said it best, *"Religion is for people who're afraid of going to hell. Spirituality is for those who've already been there."* And if there is a place called Hell—a concept, it appears, we've completely misunderstood from the source material—then it's more likely we're already in it, temporarily separated from the direct presence of God. In my own life, I've been there. I know what that feels like. But I wasn't sent there; I took myself, through my choices alone.

All that being said, I believe in the core message of Jesus Christ, and of every other religion and spiritual tradition for that matter, that love is the most important thing in life, in the universe, in death, and in every other element of the human experience. I won't subscribe to the message of do this…*or else.* I believe everyone will be redeemed: every child loved, every child fed, and every child rescued. *My message is simple—if you want to sell something, sell me on how to live, not on how to die.* I've experienced many beautiful things because of my faith, but I've also come to a pretty obvious conclusion, that there's a lot of bullshit out there, a lot of hot air—pun 100 percent intended! And we preach it to ourselves. So, if the devil isn't there to pull our strings, to tease out the worst in us, and Hell isn't the place we arrive after the proving ground called life, what then? Where does evil originate and why does it exist?

Maybe the answer can be found in the philosophy of solipsism, which states that only one's mind—my mind—is certain to exist, and that the outside world, anything outside of one's own mind, might not actually be real in the traditional, material sense. I wrestled with this as a young person, the "realness" of other people's consciousness and experience. Was it actually real? How do others perceive the world? Is their perception more right or wrong than my own?

Metaphysically speaking, solipsism asserts that there's no independent existence, that the consciousness of others simply isn't present. And if they're not present, then maybe the evil I see in the world is also not present? And since I haven't experienced a large degree of suffering and evil in my own life, then maybe I'm meant to observe and learn from evil, but not to experience it personally. Maybe, in that construct, evil is not actually happening to anyone, or being felt, which somehow makes it okay. However, this is an extremely selfish position to take, and it devalues the seemingly real experiences others are having, that they're some ghostly figments of my imagination. So, no. Not a good explanation.

Maybe the answer can be found in simulation theory, a close cousin of solipsism, that we're all just running around in some hyper-realistic video game—The Matrix. The base reality, or player one, is me, and everyone else is just a role-playing character in my little world. The game would have danger and mystery and bad things would happen, but never too much that it would cause me to quit. I wouldn't give up and I'd continue trying to solve the riddle, obsessively even. Sound familiar? Maybe the game would be optimized somehow, that if I made the right moves, I'd end up winning the game, or serving its greater purpose. Maybe my game has me being a successful author? Again, player one is the only conscious entity in this scenario, and evil and suffering are not directly experienced, not with the severity that they're observed.

I'm placed in a scary place to achieve an end goal, but I don't experience the evil and suffering I see, it's just an element of the game. Death is also not a big deal, because we can always spawn a new version of ourselves. We can hit reset. But again, this is extremely dismissive of the apparent reality of others. So, no. Not a good explanation, either. But it's fascinating to think about.

Maybe the answer can be found in the many worlds interpretation of quantum theory, that we live an infinite number of parallel lives based on each and every observation and decision we make in life (vastly simplified of course), a concept popularized in many books, most recently in *The Midnight Library* by Matt Haig. Maybe we're actually conscious in only one of those lives, but that every possibility that could occur does, yet we remain veiled from seeing those firsthand. These scenarios, or alternate realities, would infer a level of optimization just like in simulation theory. MIT computer scientist and author of *The Simulation Hypothesis* and *The Simulated Multiverse*, Rizwan Virk, concludes the later with this: *"Having taken other roads might have led to other destinations in the garden of forking paths, but we are in this particular one for some reason. There is some aspect of this life that is optimal for us, because a lot of branches of the tree may have been tried, but our player, or the quantum computing algorithm that is running the simulation, has decided what might make us less happy.... And perhaps that is the perspective that I would like to leave with you with when trying to answer these big, almost unanswerable questions. If you are in this timeline, don't worry about the other possible presents that may be existing, may have already existed, or may exist in the future. One way or another, you will most likely end up in the best possible one.* "[3] Again, fascinating subject and theory, and if I thought only about myself and my own existence, this perspective might make a lot of sense.

Maybe a hyper-advanced civilization has figured out how to create a simulation that is indistinguishable from reality? Maybe they discovered that death is real, and the simulation is a way to cheat death, to avoid real pain and suffering, to avoid evil, yet still preserve the appearance of life—of freedom and love? Maybe we're back to the garden after all, the perfect world? But I have a hard time believing a victim of the Holocaust would feel the same way, that their life in a concentration camp was optimal or simulated for some reason. That was a real thing that happened to a real person. So, no. Not a good explanation.

---

3   Rizwan Virk, *The Simulated Multiverse* (USA: Bayview Books, LLC, 2021).

Maybe there's no God at all, no purpose to the universe, and this is all a cosmic role of the dice—atheism in its purest form. In my general ignorance, I must acknowledge that's a possibility, but that would also require an intellectual concession that greatly exceeds the one that established Hell. Creation *ex nihilo*, out of nothing, is a stretch even for the most astute physicists. On the other hand, intelligent design is almost undeniable. The probabilities involved in human evolution as function of natural selection are absurd. The most often used analogy is similar to the likelihood of a hurricane blowing through a junkyard and somehow creating a working 747 jumbo jet. And isn't it something, as twentieth-century philosopher Alan Watts once said that human beings represent the most complex machines in the known universe, and yet we require very little training in how to operate them? That the billions of particles that make up our bodies just magically know what do to, that somehow inorganic and inert stardust somehow became aware of itself. Whether it was God or the universe, it took something incredibly intelligent to make us—living, sentient beings—and for some purpose. They didn't go through all that time and energy and space for nothing. So, no. No God is also not a good answer.

Maybe evil exists because it has to, because the world wouldn't be as beautiful without it. Perhaps the contrast between good and evil is the only thing that draws us to the light, draws us closer to our true essence, and that's love. This is the universal duality of the Yin and the Yang. Maybe we wouldn't recognize love if it weren't for evil? Maybe love is so important in the grand design, that we're given the freedom to do anything to preserve it? Most of us would say that we're not capable of evil, that we don't have it in us to hurt another human being, and hurt with impunity. I disagree.

Imagine if your child was strapped to a chair with a bomb around their neck—on a countdown timer. Sitting next to them is the only person in the world who knows how to diffuse it but is refusing to do so. What would you do? If that hypothetical bothers you, then how about this one: Sacrifice your child to save a billion people. What would you do?

I've surveyed dozens of people, ordinary people, on these two questions. Not one has ever said they wouldn't do anything to free their child, inflicting whatever pain or torment is necessary, resorting to torture—the lowest form of human cruelty. And interestingly enough, I give them the option of *"by any means necessary,"* which includes a lot of other possibilities besides torture, and yet they default to that immediately, going right to the bottom. And not one has ever said they'd make that sacrifice, even to save a billion, to avoid the suffering many others would experience by losing a friend, a loved one, or a child of their own. Maybe Meatloaf said it best, *"I would do anything for love."* He's right. We would do anything to protect what we love most, but too often that's not love itself, it's the shiny objects we see in the world, the things we think give us freedom: money, power, control, land, and a stronghold on individual salvation. So this answer is close, but we're not there yet.

In my opinion, evil exists for only one reason. It exists because we've been given the greatest gift in the world: freedom. And I'm not talking about free will. I'm talking about freedom of thought. We're free to think about whatever we want, whenever we want, and that freedom is never taken away. Therefore, our thoughts become our reality. They become our experience of the world. They become life as we know it. They are the ultimate choice and the ultimate responsibility.

How often are we held accountable for our thoughts? Never. We're only held accountable for our actions. There's a big difference. Envy, greed, entitlement, bitterness, arrogance, hatred, ego, selfishness, lust, control, malaise, the list goes on and on, and they all originate in our thoughts alone. They originate in our thoughts because we've made a poor choice with the information we're presented. So take responsibility for the gift of freedom, of thought. Left unchecked at personal level, well, we know where that leads.

Someone or something loved us so much that they gave us that freedom, knowing it had a terrible consequence—that if enough people thought a certain way, enormous evils could result. Often times, evil only requires the dark thoughts of one, evidenced by the phenomenon of the mass shootings of the twenty-first century. This chapter was finished on the same day as the massacre at Robb Elementary School in Uvalde, Texas, where a lone gunman killed nineteen children and two adults. It was the deadliest shooting at a U.S. school since a gunman killed twenty children and six adults at Sandy Hook Elementary in Newtown, Connecticut, in December 2012. Coincidentally, both gunman were teenagers and they both killed the person closest to them on their way to the massacre, their grandmother and mother, respectively. Something has to change, and it's the way we think. We need to take responsibility for our own anger.

At the same time, given that we have enormous capability for evil, God and the universe didn't want us to be contained. They wanted us to be unlimited, infinite—just like them. They wanted us to be free. They wanted us to have this thing called choice. That the other greatest gift in the universe is love—a choice in itself. Our thoughts alone are the origin of evil, but they don't have to be. So don't fill your heart and mind with garbage. Don't believe everything people tell you. Don't make concessions with human truth. You're smarter than that. Use your gift, and take responsibility for your thoughts—hold yourself accountable for what you think about, because no one else can or will. And, very simply, don't put bad things in your head. In his post-apocalyptic story, *The Road*, Cormac McCarthy said, *"Just remember that the things you put in your head are there forever...you forget what you want to remember and you remember what you want to forget."*

If you see a silhouette in a window, or something else on your journey from here to there, give it a little more time. Allow it to change the way you think—your thoughts. Allow it to change your life. Make that choice. In that process, you'll change others' lives as well and you'll begin to make a difference in a new way.

Start to see ordinary things for what they really are, small miracles. Find your way through the landscape that is your own mind and find the markers, the ordinary people and scenes that play out in front of you every day. Take responsibility for your thoughts and keep your eyes open, even in the darkness. Had that yoga studio been filled with light, I might not have seen that silhouette the same way.

CHAPTER 13

THE FOUR HORSEMEN

"The mind is its own place, and in itself can make a heaven of hell, a hell of heaven."

- John Milton

There's something that an anonymous co-worker, a total stranger, a little boy 'named Rocko, and Stephen Hawking all have in common. They're four of my personal heroes. They're also all in a wheelchair, but the horse they ride is the same.

I call them the Four Horsemen because they're the harbingers of a new era in my life, a new beginning, or more appropriately, a New Jerusalem. Anathema to the apocalyptic tales of the book of Revelation in the New Testament—the false prophets, war, famine, and death that bring about the destruction of the world and the final judgment—these four people would help enable a personal restoration and direct a critical inflection in my discourse with the Divine. In other words, they'd help me become the man I wanted to be, and they'd forever change the way I talked to God.

The book of Revelation is the final book of the New Testament, and thus, the Christian Bible. It's the only apocalyptic book of the New Testament and is arguably, outside of Genesis, the most enigmatic and widely analyzed cannon in the Christian religion. It's a depiction of the end of times, the final judgment whereby Jesus returns to Earth and establishes a new order. Evil and the armies of darkness are destroyed forever, and believers are saved. Non-believers perish, along with a quarter of the world's population. It's the last showdown between good and evil.

From start to finish, Revelation is cloaked in mystery, metaphor, mythical creatures, and magnificent allegory. And there's one thing that's abundantly clear throughout—a lot of bad shit has to happen before the rise of the new order, or the creation of paradise here on Earth. The Four Horsemen are the punishments that God sends to Earth to set the stage for the final judgment, and although there are numerous interpretations of the Four Horsemen, they are generally accepted as follows: the first is a white horse, signifying the coming of the Anti-Christ, or false prophet; the second is a red horse, signifying bloodshed and war; the third is a black horse, signifying famine; and the fourth is a pale or green horse, signifying death. The fourth horseman is given the authority to kill a quarter of the world's population, and, needless to say, it's not a feel-good story; unless, of course, you believe Machiavelli that the end justifies the means.

For two thousand years, countless religious leaders, scholars, theologians, authors, cultists, and a host of crazy people have opined on—even predicted—when the end of the world will occur. To date, none of them have been right. We're still here. And like clockwork, anytime something bad happens in the world, there's certain to be a reference to the Four Horsemen and the book of Revelation. In my opinion, this is a sad and unfortunate point of view. But I believe there's a human parallel in these stories, a secondary assignment in our moral coursework. I believe Revelation is teaching us something more basic, more fundamental. Maybe, in a personal sense, it's the end of one world for the sake of another—for the sake of something better, purer, and more eternal.

In my previous readings of the book of Revelation, I always asked myself why we had to destroy life to renew it. Why do we have to end lives to save lives? By comparison, the Four Horsemen in my life begat beauty with beauty. They brought me closer to God through an acknowledgement of the greatest weapon in the world—love itself. I was inspired to be a better person through the gift of love, not through the burden of fear, and my world was not destroyed to build another. I simply built a new world by finding the beauty in it, beauty

MEMOIRS OF AN ORDINARY GUY

that many times remains unnoticed. And despite the chaotic reverie of everyday life, the Four Horsemen galloped into my heart and stomped their graceful messages on my soul. The key was to recognize them when they arrived.

THE WHITE HORSE: THE ANONYMOUS CO-WORKER

In the Book of Revelation, the White Horse symbolizes the arrival of the Anti-Christ. His purpose is to wage war on humankind and confound the multitudes with a dizzying ensemble of false prophets and spiritual untruths. He targets our primary vulnerability as rational, conscious beings, which is our search for truth and meaning. It's an attack on our core identity as individuals, and the goal is confusion, making it difficult for us to understand basic questions, such as: *Who am I? What do I believe?* and *What's my purpose?* I recognized some years ago if I didn't have honest, faith-based answers to those questions, I'd never find what I was looking for in life. A phrase from Shakespeare's *Hamlet* would routinely surface in my mind: "To thine own self be true."

For most of my life, I based happiness and meaning on things that are, undoubtedly, impermanent: financial stability, health, intelligence, fitness, style, likability, a nice home, and meaningful relationships. These are important endeavors, and it's wise to place a certain emphasis on these things. However, given their impermanence, should they drive our happiness?

My perspective would change almost instantly upon my first encounter with the White Horse when I asked myself, for the first time, if I could be happy if those things we're taken away. What level of physical and material reduction could my happiness withstand? Could I still find joy and maintain a positive attitude when the things I hold dearest are pulled from my mortal grip? I'd grown accustomed to winning, but was I prepared to lose?

I remember watching a disabled woman from our accounting department in the parking lot below my window at work. At the time, I was in my mid-thirties and working as a finance professional for a defense contractor in Northern Virginia. Things were going well. I had a good job, and I also had two young twins that I adored, and I was generally happy. Or so I thought.

As this woman pulled into the parking lot, I first felt a subtle amazement at how technology can assist those with disabilities and how it can bring a sense of normal to an otherwise abnormal set of circumstances. Her car had been modified so she could safely drive with only the use of her hands. She was paralyzed from the waist down.

I watched her for several minutes as she performed the otherwise routine, getting out of her car, an action I've negotiated thousands of times without second thought. Even from a distance and a height of twenty feet, her movements seemed tedious and physically exhausting, no doubt a workout in themselves. I witnessed gravity playing a cruel tug of war with her lifeless legs and her trembling arms and shoulders. Her face struggled to hide a long history of frustration and unwanted challenges—gravity of a different sort.

Time seemed to stop, as if I were living her life in slow motion. Immediately, I considered the simple tasks in her life that must be far more difficult than mine, and I vowed something in her honor. You'll probably never hear me say, "I had a hard day." You'll certainly never hear me complain. Happiness, and my identity in life, instantly took on a new meaning. They'd never again be grounded in the groundless, in baseless materialism or ego, but in something more basic, something more eternal.

My perspective would never be the same. She forced a most important question. Could I be happy if things started to go wrong in my life, if major changes started to occur? And I finally acknowledged that change is a veiled certainty in mortal life. It's something we most often forget and try our best to avoid. But we're tasked to be happy at every stage of our lives regardless of loss and regardless of change. In that instant—looking out my window with my arms crossed and head down—I knew I had to build a new foundation; I needed to find new bedrock, impervious to the shifting sands of the corporeal world. That bedrock would be love, faith, and the eternal progress of my soul; and if I lived for those three, things would always be okay.

The White Horse helped me recognize the thoughts and actions that antagonized my eternal identity—mainly the shallow massaging of my ego and the temptations and false expectations of the material world, as well as other people. I'd also set a new standard for self-honesty, one that would fill my faith journey with clarity and an empowered consecration to simple truths: love, gratitude, compassion, and my ultimate union with the Divine. I'd learn to define those elements for myself, through my own moral endeavor. To me, that endeavor is brutal self-honesty and a fearless march toward something higher.

This experience reminds me of another of my favorite quotes from Thoreau's *Walden*:

> I know of no more encouraging fact than the unquestionable ability of man to elevate his life by a conscious endeavor. It is something to be able to paint a particular picture, or to carve a statue, and so to make a few objects beautiful; but it is far more glorious to carve and paint the very atmosphere and medium through which we look, which morally we can do. To affect the quality of the day, that is the highest of arts.[4]

The chapter is entitled "Where I Lived, and What I Lived For." My temporal atmosphere, the constant rhetoric, noise,

---

4   Henry David Thoreau, *Walden*, 1854.

and information warfare we see all around us now seemed manufactured, ancillary, and unnecessary. The real atmosphere, the one which Thoreau was referring to, was the temple I'd start re-building from within. It was the revival of my soul and a re-building of my spiritual base. And it all started with a three-minute pause at my window at work, watching someone who was far stronger than I was with a spiritual engine that outworked mine in every way.

The Anti-Christ was never an individual for me, it wasn't Satan or a punishment from God. The White Horse was a warning that my spiritual progression was stalling. The Anti-Christ was a false identity and a swarm of personal deceptions that defiled who I thought I was and who I thought I should be—at its core, a debasement of my soul. The Anti-Christ was also an internal demon, one that I'd learn to silence and conquer over time. I was reminded, through an otherwise random and simple encounter on just another average day, that although I lived in material abundance, I was spiritually poor and penniless in the currency of the Divine. The White Horse would, ultimately, help destroy an old world in favor of another.

THE RED HORSE: A TOTAL STRANGER

There's a civil war being fought inside all of us, and the battleground is our mind. Our thoughts can be our greatest savior but also our worst adversary. I spent a lot of my life worrying about things that never actually happened, and I've felt sorry for myself for things that the rest of the world would feel lucky to have. Looking back, I consider this a tragic misuse of my time on Earth and woeful atrophy of my eternal progress.

But nonetheless, I'm human. I'm vulnerable to worry, suffering, and pain just like anybody. There'll no doubt be great challenges at every stage of my life. There'll also be great successes. And the question I'll have to ask myself when my days conclude is how I responded to both. How well did I actually live? How well did I handle success and failure? How did I treat others? What kind of person was I really, and how will I be remembered? And most importantly, what did I learn?

As humans, we have a gift in mortal life, the gift of choice. We can choose how we fight the battle. We can fight it with a smile or with a frown, it's that simple. Like anything, there are major exceptions to the simple rules, but for most of us, it's our attitude that largely drives our experience, both good and bad. It's how we view the world that determines our behavior and experience in it. We can face life's challenges with courage, hope, and a belief in the eternal, or we can simply live to die another day. It's how we respond that determines our happiness. It's about the choices we make, and I choose to respond with a smile.

One of my favorite things to do is to smile at a total stranger. In fact, I smile, or at least nod, at everyone I pass wherever I go. It doesn't matter whether I'm out on a run, in the grocery store, at the gym, or simply walking from here to there. I've always felt it was the right thing to do. To not acknowledge someone's presence always seemed rude to me, even as a small child. It's a simple gesture that requires no effort, but it can change somebody's day in an instant, especially if it's genuine.

Sometimes I'll encounter someone who's obviously having a tough time and looks frustrated or appears to be suffering in one way or another. They often have their head down to avoid such contact, but I can usually draw their attention. And while the gesture is unexpected and can be somewhat awkward initially, I rarely find where their expression doesn't immediately change. A simple acknowledgement of their presence, perhaps where it has gone unnoticed for too long, is enough to completely change their attitude, and thus their experience, if only for an instant. Perhaps this momentary lift will ripple through their day. Maybe they'll go home and hug a loved one a little tighter or treat a spouse with greater love and respect. Perhaps it'll soften their heart and provide a glimpse of something greater. I believe we can change the world with a smile. Or at a minimum, it can change our attitude which then changes our experience of the world.

There's a wonderful scene in the movie *Gladiator*. In the film, Maximus Decimus Meridius, played by Russell Crowe, is a Roman general who's betrayed by the son of emperor Marcus Aurelius. Upon hearing the news that he'll not succeed his father as emperor, Commodus, played by Joaquin Phoenix, murders his father and seizes the throne. Knowing Maximus will be suspicious, Commodus orders his execution and has his family murdered.

Maximus survives the execution attempt but is injured in the process and is later captured by a traveling horde of slave owners. He then finds himself as sword fodder in various gladiator games, but, through his military skills and leadership as a general, he ascends the ranks and eventually returns to Rome to perform in the great Colosseum. Intent on revenge for the murder of his family and the former emperor, Maximus secretly plots against Commodus. His plan is eventually foiled, and Maximus ends up face-to-face with Commodus in a dungeon of the great arena in a pivotal scene at the end of the movie. In order to regain the approval of the people, who are now chanting Maximus's name from above, Commodus challenges Maximus in a fight to the death. To gain an advantage, Commodus stabs Maximus and conceals the wound prior to the challenge, but, needless to say, Maximus eventually wins the duel. But it's their exchange in the dungeon that's the most powerful scene of the movie. It is perhaps my favorite scene in any movie:

COMMODUS: Maximus. Maximus. Maximus. They call for you. The general who became a slave. The slave who became a gladiator. The gladiator who defied an emperor. Striking story. Now the people want to know how the story ends. Only a famous death will do. And what could be more glorious than to challenge the emperor himself in the great arena.

COMMODUS: You would fight me?

COMMODUS: Why not? Do you think I'm afraid?

COMMODUS: I think you've been afraid all your life.

COMMODUS: Unlike Maximus the Invincible, who knows no fear?

MAXIMUS [laughing]: I knew a man once who said death smiles at us all. All a man can do is smile back.[5]

Just smile back. It was perhaps the greatest analogy I'd ever heard on how to live. Smile at life's challenges in the same manner as its triumphs, just as Rudyard Kipling said in his famous poem "If": "If you can meet with Triumph and Disaster and treat those two impostors just the same...."

After all, maybe it wasn't about conquering the fear of death or the unknown or any of the petty kingdoms that existed in my little world. It was about the death of fear, the real adversary. If I was going to be at peace, I needed to learn that fear could no longer dominate my thoughts, that the

---

5   Scott, Ridley, director. *Gladiator*. 2000; Universal City, CA: DreamWorks SKG. 155 min.

incessant warfare of internal worry was curable, and the suffering that resulted was a choice. Just smile back—a lesson that'd be taught again many years later by the Red Horse.

I was driving to work one morning and saw a little boy and his mother on their way to school. It caught my attention because he was riding on the handlebars of her electric wheelchair. It became very clear to me in that moment that I needed to pause and watch. I remember the smiles on their faces. I remember how they hugged each other. I remember the love and deep affection between them. As I sat there, I felt a little depressed and worried about certain aspects of my life. But in that moment, I realized something profound. Clearly, there were some circumstances in this woman's life that were very different from mine. And if she can smile, then so can I. On an ordinary fall morning, I received the unexpected gift of a lifetime.

I'm grateful that I'm not in a wheelchair; my problems are trivial compared to those of so many others. The beauty was not in the perspective or in the comparison between me and another. The beauty was in the lesson learned: that regardless of what happens, the choice—how I respond—is mine. Just smile back.

THE BLACK HORSE: A LITTLE BOY NAMED ROCKO

The Black Horse in the book of Revelation signals the onset of a global famine, one resulting from the warfare and carnage brought on by the previous two riders. But I don't believe this is a punishment from God or a description of a real event. It's not a global calamity. I believe it's a page taken from the Lord's playbook—his eternal game plan for this thing called life. Jesus spoke in parables so that we might ponder deeply the meaning of his messages and apply them in our own lives. They're open for interpretation, and they mean different things to different people. Therefore, works such as Revelation, I maintain, deserve the same level of intellectual and personal discovery.

I believe the Black Horse is hinting at something deeper, and, at the same time, something more basic. I believe it's alluding to a spiritual famine, a personal starvation of the essential element—the one God wants us to feed on the most. That essential element is love. I'm an optimist, and, as such, I believe there's inherently more good in most of us than there is evil. However, living a life of love requires our constant attention and action. Otherwise, we can quickly fall short of the Lord's expectation—one of his two greatest commandments in the New Testament—to love your neighbor as you would yourself. To fully embrace love in our lives requires effort and, in itself, is a choice we make every day, with everybody. It can and should be a question we ask ourselves often: Am I filling the world with more love or am I not? It's pretty simple.

To physically survive, we need food and water. But to really live, be happy, find comfort, face the unknown, and progress toward the infinite, we need love. We need to feel it deeply and place it at the center of everything we do. We need to know there's someone "out there" who loves us, and that basic need for love doesn't diminish with age, health, maturity, success, money, or any of the other material measures of our earthly transience. At every point in our lives, we need an advocate, and we need love—a lesson I'd re-learn on Memorial Day 2020.

Rocko was a fourteen-year-old boy who I met at a Memorial Day barbecue at a friend's house in Northern Virginia. Only a couple weeks later did I learn his name, but when I saw him for the first time, I was stunned by his presence. There was something about him that made it very difficult for me to look away. In the few hours I spent with him, I knew he'd become an important teacher in my life. That being said, I've had a decent amount of life experience. I've had a lot of very smart people and mentors teach me all kinds of different things. I've read and gained perspective from many, many works and authors. But without speaking a word—because he couldn't—Rocko re-taught me one of life's basic lessons. In fact, he and his father taught it better than anyone.

Rocko and his family arrived at the barbecue shortly after we did, and I had already posted up on the back deck prior to their arrival. It was a beautiful spring day, and I was enjoying the company of friends and family. As I was leaning against the wood railing of the deck, and amidst a small shuffle of people inside, I noticed something unexpected—a small boy in a wheelchair. He was dressed in all black and seemed to blend into the darkness of the kitchen and the sharp glare and reflections of the sliding glass door. It was quickly apparent that Rocko had a lot of challenges, and only later did I notice the straps on his legs and chest. Many of the freedoms we take for granted, even the freedom of movement, were not the same for Rocko. For most of us, being strapped to a chair, with little or no ability to move, would be a form of torture. My heart immediately softened.

His father wheeled him onto the back deck to within an arm's length of me, and that's where they'd stay for the remainder of the afternoon. Rocko had a simple, yet curious expression that I found a bit mysterious. His gaze was somewhat subdued but purposeful, and the whites of his eyes were crystal clear—something of a paradox. He was captivating, and it was something deeper inside him that connected us. I couldn't look away, and I wanted to know more.

I wondered what he was thinking. What did he perceive of the world around him? I wondered if he knew he was disabled and if he felt emotional pain and frustration as a result. Did he understand basic things? How did he communicate his needs? He didn't speak a word, but that also didn't seem to be an option. It was clear that his knowledge and experience of the world were extremely limited. But I couldn't get the thought out of mind. *What did he experience?* Later that afternoon I'd get my answer, and it would change me forever.

Rocko's father never left his side. I watched as he gently caressed his son's hand for hours, a simple act that, I believe, confirmed for Rocko that he wasn't alone, that he was loved, and that his father would always be there for him. It confirmed for him that he had an advocate, and I was mesmerized by the simple and magnificent exchange between a father and son. Occasionally, Rocko's father would stop rubbing his hand, but, after a few seconds in the absence of this contact, Rocko would perform an action that I'll never forget. He'd simply look up, and his father would continue. In his own way, Rocko knew how to love. He also knew the absence of that love and how to reconnect with it when it faded away. He knew how to connect with someone and what that meant to himself personally.

Rocko's basic needs were met. He was complete: food, water, and love. That's all we truly need. And whether we look up, look within, find it through prayer, read it in a book, or see it on a deck one spring day, God's love is always there for us. And just like Rocko's father, God gently rubs our hand with the thing we need most.

My experience with Rocko and his father reaffirmed my testimony of love. It's the language of the universe. It's something everyone can understand and feel. And it's something we all need. Without it, we die. Rocko struck my heart and conscience with a profound clarity. His message was loud and clear: *Always remember me, and always remember love.*

THE PALE HORSE: STEPHEN HAWKING

I'll close by telling you about another of my personal heroes. Physicist Stephen Hawking was arguably one of the greatest minds in all of human history. But at the age of twenty-one, he was diagnosed with ALS (or Lou Gehrig's disease), a progressive neurodegenerative disease which ultimately results in total paralysis from the decay and death of neurons in the brain and spinal cord. At the time, doctors gave him two years to live. He'd eventually exceed those expectations by over fifty years, and as the disease progressed, he'd lose the ability to walk, speak, and eventually to move at all. He'd spend the last forty years of his life in a wheelchair and, for most of that time, would communicate through the use of a computer program that produced his famously anachronistic and mechanical voice. He died on March 9, 2018.

Below is an excerpt from his last book *Brief Answers to the Big Questions*. It was published posthumously, seven months after his death. The afterword was written by his daughter, Lucy. I've read many great things in my life, words that have rattled the deepest parts of my soul, but none more so than these: "My father never gave up; he never shied away from the fight. At the age of seventy-five, completely paralysed and able to move only a few facial muscles, he still got up every day, put on a suit and went to work."[6]

In a simple, eloquent statement, Lucy defined what kind of man her father was and how she felt about him. I can only hope that my children will say the same about me upon my death. Mr. Hawking was everything I want to be. He was a fighter, a physicist, a free thinker, and a visionary. He had every reason to give up, every reason to complain and feel sorry for himself. He had every reason to say it was too hard. But he didn't. Even in his crippled state, he made significant contributions to science and would fundamentally change how we viewed the world in many ways. He inspired others, and for me, he'd represent—by contrast—the death of my old ways and would become a cornerstone in the new temple that I'd begin building from the ground up.

The Four Horsemen are just several of my heroes. They helped me blaze new trails—four new paths to happiness I hadn't traveled before. Their lessons were simple. If I was honest with myself and focused on my eternal progress, if I smiled in the face of tribulation, if I put love at the center of everything I did and feasted on its fruits, and if I never gave up, then the New Jerusalem would eventually descend from the heavens. One day, I'll enter its gates as something different— the man I know I can be.

---

6   Stephen Hawking, *Brief Answers to the Big Questions* (NY: Bantam Books, 2018).

CHAPTER 14

THE COKE

"Everything which is done in the present, affects the future by consequence, and the past by redemption."

- Paulo Coelho

The following story was written by my dad. At the time of its writing—the summer of 2020—he was seventy-five years old and living in Marco Island, Florida. It was one of the joys of my life to work on this story with him and to help bring its beautiful message to life once again. It was a moment I wish I'd had more of. He told me this story was the most memorable experience of his life. I believe him.

It was 1968 and it was hot, really hot. This was not unusual for the month of July in South Vietnam. I'd just gotten off a CH-46 helicopter along with a platoon of Marines. Our position was on Route 9, a dirt road, which traversed the country in the northern provinces and was about ten miles east of the former combat base of Khe Sanh (the siege of Khe Sanh had already been lifted during Operation Pegasus in the months prior). I was the platoon's commander and brand new to the platoon. I was also new "in-country." We were combat engineers, and our mission was to provide engineering support to the Third Battalion Fourth Marines (3/4). Specifically, our mission was to construct pads and emplacements for an incoming battery of M102 105mm howitzer cannons. The howitzers would be located at 3/4's forward headquarters on top of the mountain that now stood above us.

Our task was vital to the safety and success of the Third Marine Division as they pushed westward toward the Laotian border. Infantry units were already at the western edge of their artillery's effective range, and our mission needed to be accomplished as soon as possible. Our location was in bad guy country, but it was still relatively secure. Further west was not so secure.

Because of circumstances, we had to climb the mountain with all of our combat gear and engineering tools and explosives; the helicopter couldn't deposit us on the top. So, as platoon commander, my first job was to get everyone and our equipment up the hill. I hadn't met any of the men except for the platoon sergeant.

We crossed a small bridge, over a stream parallel to Route 9, and then started up the mountain. In some places it was so steep that we had to grab at foliage to keep from falling back down the mountain. All of us were carrying our field packs and weapons, and we teamed up to help move the heavier gear. I was helping carry a large metal box. We were ladened down, and it was painful going in the heat and humidity. After half an hour—and midway up the mountain—I told the platoon sergeant to tell the men to take a break. When we stopped, I looked in the box and saw a single can of Coca-Cola. On impulse, I opened the can and drank the Coke. A few minutes later, we resumed our climb. Up until now the men had been noisy—lots of good-natured griping and the usual goofing around. But for the remainder of the trip, they were noticeably quiet.

We reached the top and proceeded to dig in and get our gear in order. I reported in to the 3/4 commanding officer and, after that, checked in with my platoon sergeant to see how everything was going. In our conversation, I mentioned that I noticed the men seemed a little sullen and not very responsive to me. I said I thought that was odd in that we hadn't really had a chance to meet and get acquainted with one another. With due respect, he hesitated and then explained why. The Coke I drank was theirs, and the only one. When we reached the top of the hill and secured our position, there was to be a platoon drawing for it. I was mortified that I had done something so terribly thoughtless.

It took some time to regain their good will and confidence, but soon all was forgiven and forgotten. But not for me. My action left a lasting and profound impact on me. Fifty-two years later, I still think about that scene, especially if I'm in a meal line or about to retrieve something to drink from the fridge. I think about how such a truly minor event lives so long in my memory.

The obvious lesson would seem to be "don't be selfish," but to me there's much more here than just a lesson. My thoughtless act created a remembrance, an indelible kind of memory to which there's an inescapable obligation. The often-present thoughts of the unflagging good cheer and loyalty of those men from a long time ago is my remembrance. It ties me to them with an obligation to not forget my mistake, and to not forget them.

I love his story. To me, it's a simple and powerful example of atonement, redemption, and love. My father made a mistake. He recognized something wasn't right and sought out an answer. An advocate then came to his aid, and my dad did his best to make things right. And through a process of forgiveness, he was reunited with those he loved and those who loved him. I love you, Dad! Thank you!

CHAPTER 15

THE GIANT

*"To be yourself in a world that is constantly trying to
make you something else is the greatest accomplishment."*

- Ralph Waldo Emerson

The first half of this book has a religious theme, and now I'd like to transition to a more secular and temporal narrative. I'll tell you about some experiences I've had through a lens I believe we all share regardless of our faith—the human lens. And it all starts with a period of intense personal reflection, a short period of time I spent on the shoulders of a giant.

That morning I had a goal. I didn't care how hard I had to work or how much pain I had to endure; I was going to break my own record. I was going to ride faster than I had before, and I was going to push the limit. Tingling with excitement and energy for the adventure that lay ahead, I proceeded to take my typical morning medicine—one part English muffin with peanut butter, two parts fruit, and three parts caffeine—and then clipped into my Giant TCR1 road bike and headed out for what was sure to be a personal best, a record-breaking ride through the rolling hills and neighborhoods of Northern Virginia. It was a cool, late summer morning, one that I'd never forget.

About forty-five minutes into the ride, everything was on the right track. I was going fast, my heart rate was where it needed to be, and my energy level felt just right—more than enough to get me to the end of the ride and to a personal best. My feat hammered away at the pedals, and my mind and body were focused squarely on my goal. I was in "the zone," a state of flow that most athletes experience at one point or another. The best I can describe is that it was a state of non-thought, the space between the conscious and the unconscious, where the effort becomes effortless, and it was where I needed to be.

But shortly thereafter, my mind started to drift to the thoughts and worries of any common day. I started thinking about my business, about the coronavirus, about my children's education, and a dozen things that were on my to-do list. I also realized something else. I was now going noticeably slower. The wind in my face wasn't quite as strong. My feet weren't hammering the pedals like they had before. My heart rate had dropped significantly, and my breathing was noticeably easier.

A cold chill ran through my body as I looked down at the speedometer—bad news. The questions immediately followed. How long had it been? How much did this loss of concentration set me back? How much time had I lost? At that point, I knew I'd made a grave error. I blew it. I estimated that I was out of "the zone" for about three minutes. And despite my best efforts for the remainder of the ride, I'd fail to achieve my goal. But those three minutes—what amounted to a 5 percent distraction—would end up changing everything. That failed goal caused me, a short time later, to reflect on the other failings of my life, the perceived weaknesses I had. As a result, I started the process of chasing a new goal, a heightened priority on what really mattered to me: understanding who I truly was.

At every stage of my life, I've felt a bit inadequate. I didn't like some aspect of myself. I tried to avoid who I really was, and I felt uncomfortable in my own skin. What a tragedy! When I was in elementary school, I felt like my family didn't have a whole lot of money, which was actually true. My father was a civil servant for the US Department of Agriculture, which wasn't a particularly high-paying job at the time, and my mother was a substitute teacher and worked at a local thrift store, giving free clothes to people in the community. It's also where she bought clothes for me, for pennies on the dollar. An annual trip to the big-name department store for back-to-school shopping wasn't an option in my house. And even though the clothes from the thrift shop were beautiful, they weren't new. They were used. They didn't cost a whole lot of money, and I was extremely self-conscious about that. I never admitted that to anyone. When someone would ask me where I got a shirt or a sweater or something else I was wearing, I'd make something up—I'd lie—or quickly change the subject.

I remember the countless times I stood in front of the closet, trying to figure out which combination of clothes would make me look the richest. I remember the anxiety. I remember the shame. And I remember the fear that I wouldn't be one of the cool kids if I didn't look the part. We didn't have a whole lot of extra cash, but I grew up in a beautiful house. We had a boat (which was an antique and given to us by my grandfather), and I had all the things a little boy would ever want. I never went without. And yet I felt poor, because I never had new clothes. There was something about clothing that drove my identity and self-worth.

When I was in high school, I was skinny. Skinny might not even be the right word. As a freshman, I was 5'10" and 110 pounds, about halfway under the "healthy" line on any Body Mass Index (BMI) chart. I vividly remember my freshman basketball picture—not an ounce of muscle and thin as a rail. I felt weak, and everywhere I looked, my peers seemed bigger and stronger than me. As a result, I'd wear three to four undershirts to make myself look bigger. I'd buy shoes that were two sizes too big. My jeans were baggy—not because that was in style but to hide my skinny legs from the world. I also developed very late and, needless to say, I avoided the showers at all costs. I held a knife in the gun fight, outmatched in every way, or so I thought.

When I was in college—and still very thin—I didn't feel desirable to women. I was terrified of my own sexuality and was also profoundly introverted, lacking a particularly loud or macho demeanor. I had a picture in my mind of what women wanted, and I wasn't it. I avoided having a girlfriend because I lacked self-confidence as a man, as a protector, and I didn't believe I possessed the strength, emotional presence, and physical maturity that a functional human relationship required. In short, I just didn't think I had "it." And because I didn't have "it," I didn't have it—sex that is. I was a virgin until I was twenty-eight.

When I reached the workforce as a business consultant for PricewaterhouseCoopers, I was woefully unprepared. I was a biology major in college, so inept in the ways of Microsoft Office and even basic business principles that I couldn't calculate formulas in Excel or a simple profit and loss statement. The business and consulting lingo was like a foreign language. You might ask how I landed at a Big 5 consulting firm as a biology major. Well, I got lucky. My uncle was the Chief Operating Officer of my business unit and helped me get an internship two years prior. My first job was working for the building facilities manager over a winter break from college. They were moving offices and needed some help placing partner and senior level managers in their respective offices. On my first day as an "intern," I was handed a set of blueprints and a box of crayons. My job was to color code the partner and manager offices—probably all that I was qualified for at the time.

The internship came at a very critical time. I wasn't doing well in college, and now I was guaranteed a job with the Big 5 when I graduated. On the flip side, I was slowly abandoning everything I ever wanted to do. I wanted to be a physicist, but I'd taken the easy road, the guaranteed path. I remember with total clarity the morning on my first day of work. I pulled up to a stop sign a couple miles from my house and felt a deep sense of fear and disappointment that not only did I have forty to fifty more years of work ahead of me, I also wasn't following my heart; this wasn't where I wanted to be. I knew that pursuing my dream of being a physicist was dwindling quickly. In reality, I knew it was over. I hadn't put myself on the right path. PricewaterhouseCoopers sounded prestigious; it sounded smart, like I had done something right. But, in fact, I'd done everything wrong.

When I returned to church for the first time in eight years, I found myself at odds with even the most basic tenets of the Christian faith. Many issues still exist today. I don't believe in the Garden of Eden. I don't believe in original sin. I don't believe in Noah's Ark. I don't believe in a "young" Earth. I don't believe in miracles as they are typically described. I don't believe God punishes the wicked and rewards the faithful. I don't believe that obedience leads to prosperity. I don't understand—with any sort of rational completeness—why Jesus had to suffer a horrible death because of my imperfections. I don't believe in Hell (obviously). And I certainly don't believe it is the eternal destination for non-believers. Whatever church doors I step through—and I've stepped through many—I don't fit in. I end up the contrarian, the renegade, and the guy who tends to say "Yeah, but…" as opposed to "I believe."

Maybe it's just the way I'm wired, and my lack of belief in basic Christian doctrine doesn't seem to be waning. It probably never will. And yet I find myself with a greater passion for the life and ministry of Jesus Christ than ever before. His message, his life, his service, and his personal sacrifice draw an energy from somewhere deep inside me. This energy is a reminder of my eternal origin and my basic nature as a spiritual being. But I believe the energy inside me has many names: the quantum, the source, the Brahman, the Atman, the light, and many others I've yet to discover. There seem to be many paths—one for each of us. And my spiritual quest has just begun.

When I got married, I feared having someone around all the time. I feared having to be that present with another human being, that I always had to be "on" so to speak. I'm an only child and used to being alone. I feared my introversion and the aloofness of my wandering thoughts and daydreams wouldn't be understood by someone else—even my wife. To this day, I still don't like happy hours. I don't like big gatherings and awkward social situations. I don't like shouting over a noisy crowd, small talk, forced introductions, or pretending to care about an otherwise senseless conversation. These things don't appeal to me. But I've always wondered why it seemed so easy for everyone else. Why was I so lousy in these situations? On the other hand, I've always cherished time spent in the intimate company of a few. In fact, I've thrived in these environments. But that didn't seem like a good enough trade off. I felt like there was something wrong.

At every stage of my life, I wasn't comfortable with who I was. But those three minutes on the shoulders of a giant changed everything. I realized that I was chasing the wrong goal, that the ultimate goal was to be at peace with myself, to turn my perceived weaknesses into strengths, to understand myself over everything else, and to become the person I wanted to be. The giant turned my focus to the real goals in life: faith, virtue, the protection of my character, the pursuit of knowledge, self-discipline, self-honesty, and good intent.

And like that three-minute distraction caused me to miss the mark, the world can quickly take away everything if we're not careful. It can make you something you don't want to be. It can make you believe you're something you're not. And it can take away the greatest gift you've ever received—and that's you. That in life, if we're not in "the zone" most of the time, if not always, then we can quickly miss the mark and the goals we set for ourselves. The giant taught me that I wasn't who I thought I was—the poor, skinny, undesirable, undereducated, faithless, absent, wallflower. That's what I thought the world was telling me. But I'm much more than that. And, ironically, I actually never wanted to be any of the things that I thought I wasn't. I now remember the past differently and am at peace with my experience of it—at peace with myself.

For the first time in my life, I'm completely comfortable. I know what I need to do. I want to be the greatest father in the world. I want to love another more than I love myself. I want to be as strong as I am vulnerable. I want to be faithful. I want to be a role model, a teacher, and a hero. I want to be larger than life. I want to be the greatest man in the universe and the baddest motherfucker who ever lived. Most importantly, I want to be true to myself. I just want to be me.

CHAPTER 16

THE CANADIAN

"There's no replacement for displacement."

- Walter Owen Bentley

J amie Clarke was the ninth Canadian to climb Mount Everest. He summited for the first time on May 23, 1997, at the age of twenty-nine. It was his third attempt. Bad weather and altitude sickness had forced his previous teams to turn back, the second attempt being just 150 meters from the summit. Between 1993 and 2008, he'd go on to complete the Seven Summits, the successful ascent of the tallest mountain on each of the six remaining continents. He's also one of very few Westerners to cross the Empty Quarter on camelback—a 250,000 square mile section of desert encompassing the lower third of the Arabian Peninsula.

I met Jamie in the summer of 1999, between my junior and senior years at Virginia Tech. I was an intern with PricewaterhouseCoopers (PwC) and attending the Disney

Institute in Orlando, Florida, a week-long team building and business forum for the Big 5 interns across the country. At the time, the Big 5 was comprised of Arthur Andersen, Deloitte & Touche, Ernst & Young, KPMG, and us. Jamie was the concluding motivational speaker on the last day of the conference, and he changed my life.

At the time, I was just an average student in college. I was average because I had very little passion for what I was studying. My major didn't complement my strengths and ultimate goals, but I thought it sounded good and perhaps was the path to a successful career. More so, I thought it impressed people and made me sound smart. I told people I had big plans, that my passion for biology stemmed from an out-to-work-day trip in high school with my next-door neighbor; he was my chaperone for the day at the National Cancer Institute (NCI) of the National Institutes of Health (NIH) in Bethesda, Maryland. I told people I wanted to do research, to tackle big problems like cancer or the AIDS virus. None of this was true, and it was a bad choice for many reasons. In truth, I was drawn to the mountains and the stars. I wanted to be a physicist. I wanted to be writer. And I wanted to live a life of adventure.

I was also average because I'd known since the middle of my sophomore year that I was likely guaranteed a job when I graduated. The summer before that week in Orlando, Florida, I'd completed my first internship with Coopers & Lybrand (one of the two predecessor companies prior to their merger with Price Waterhouse). I was invited to a highly competitive program for only one reason; as I stated in the previous chapter, my late uncle was the Chief Operating Officer. A biology major with average grades was not what they were looking for, and, as a result of such good fortune, my only motivation in college was to finish. I didn't need a high GPA to get a good job; I already had that. I'd bypassed any scrutiny of my actual grades. And I just needed to finish. I just needed "good enough."

I vividly remember my first day as an intern, seated at a long boardroom table with over thirty other students from across the country. It was intimidating; in fact, I only know one stronger word for it—terrifying. We started off with a couple brief welcomes and introductions by Human Resources and then from selected leaders from around the business. This was followed by a round of introductions from all of us. We were asked to say our name, school, favorite hobby, and where we'd be working that summer. Being an introvert and not particularly comfortable in front of large groups—which is ironic considering I developed a love for public speaking—even a short introduction was enough to make me feel uncomfortable. And so it started: Harvard, Yale, Northwestern, Columbia; senior partners and official sounding projects and business areas. And then me—a biology major from Virginia Tech working for the IT help desk.

Needless to say, I stuck out like a sore thumb. The guy seated to my left—who, ironically, was a close family friend of the Chief Executive Officer—asked the million-dollar question: "So who do you know?" Ouch! Was it really that obvious? Should I fess up? I was exposed in the first five minutes of day one on the job, a detail I was doing my best to hide.

The guy on my left—Mark was his name—was wearing a Façonnable dress shirt and nice slacks that fit well. He looked the part, like he belonged in the big office. I couldn't even pronounce Façonnable—I'd never seen that word before in my life—but it looked expensive, especially the fancy looking tag on the breast pocket. And for a kid who'd shopped at a second-hand store his whole life, it seemed like another world, a world away. By contrast, I was wearing a pair of kha-ki-colored Dickies. And if you don't know what Dickies are, let's just say they're designed for the jobsite, not the board-room. They actually looked halfway decent, neatly pressed with sharp lines—but they were made of rough polyester and, upon closer examination, would be a dead giveaway. They cost twenty dollars from Kmart and were hard to miss with the Dickies label above the rear pocket. Mark's second comment a little later on [chuckling] was, "Dude. Are those Dickies?" It was a great question actually; both were. The disparity of my situation was as outrageous as it was intriguing. Here I was with a pair of twenty-dollar pants, sitting in a room where the average cost of an education could easily top $200,000. If

I took anything at all from the experience, it would be gratitude. I was grateful for the opportunity. I didn't belong there.

Now in most other situations, the combination of Mark's two comments—the one-two punch calling out the inadequacy of my mere presence at the table as well as my cheap clothes—would've prompted me to look for conversation elsewhere, and permanently. But there was something unique about him, something rather charming, actually. He was like a big brother, a tough guy with a big heart. He was a man with humble beginnings but had big ideas and dreams, and he'd be my closest friend that summer. And despite the glaring contrast of our wardrobes, we were both cut from the same professional cloth. We got our start from a stroke of good fortune, exclusive purveyors in the timeless marketplace of nepotistic advantage. In other words, we were both the boss's kids. It seems unfair, and it was. But it also taught us a great lesson—and Mark would agree—that in business, relationships matter. In fact, they matter more than anything. We'd go on to be lifelong friends.

Now, as a rising senior, I'd been invited back for a second summer as an intern in the firm's proposal services department. Mark helped me get connected with the proposal team, as he had interned there the previous summer. This was key because it was a business function and I'd likely be offered a job as a consultant rather than an IT professional. Consultants generally had higher starting salaries and were billable, meaning they were profit centers for the business. It was also a better career path in my opinion. Now all I had to do now was graduate—on time.

I'd end up doing well my senior year, but only because the administrators of the College of Arts and Sciences told me I had to. They said I had to play catch-up, and quickly; I had two semesters to prove that I was worthy of a Bachelor of Science degree in biology at Virginia Tech. It was pretty binary—do these things and you'll graduate. I heard the message loud and clear. In retrospect, I was probably driven by my ego more than anything. How embarrassing would it be to have my offer rescinded because I failed to graduate? So, I did the things I needed to do, and I graduated on time. I received my offer; an offer that was guaranteed since my first day at Coopers & Lybrand three years earlier—the day I was handed that box of crayons.

In the end, I got lucky. I would've never made it to the workforce on my own effort and merit, certainly not to a firm on that level. It was the beginning of an otherwise great career, and I'll be forever grateful for the opportunity I was given. My uncle Dave made that possible. But in the end, I made some bad choices. I took the easy road. I took a shortcut, and the equivalent of a professional handout. I made a decision to not pursue my passions, and it was a white-collar death sentence. These decisions precipitated a slow decay of everything I ever wanted to do. And the worst part was that I knew it. It was a deliberate surrender.

The last day of the conference, as I sat there in that dark auditorium in a fold-out chair with my elbows on my knees, Jamie reminded me of that surrender. He reminded me of how little I'd actually worked, how little I'd earned, and just how lucky I really was. But he was inspiring beyond words. He breathed a fire into my heart that I'd never felt before. My feet bounced with excitement as I struggled to contain an energy that even made my head tingle. My heart burned with a passion for a new direction and a new life. I nurtured every second, his words my new gospel. I wanted nothing more than to follow him right out the front door of that auditorium, and I wanted nothing to do with the industry I'd found myself in. He was everything I wanted to be—an adventurer, a risk taker, a father, a motivator, a free spirit, and an inspiration to others.

He taught me one of the most important lessons of my life: there's no replacement for hard work, no shortcuts to the top, and I am limited only by the size of my motor—which is the capacity of my heart and the will of my soul. He taught me that I'd never make real progress if I didn't follow my heart and didn't take risks with myself, my emotions, my career, and my relationships—basically with everything that mattered. No risk, no reward—a simple and often repeated principle but one that I hadn't learned, much less put into practice. And it was one photograph that changed everything. It was a picture of Jamie on a treadmill during a routine workout in preparation for his third Everest attempt. On his shoulders was a ninety-pound backpack. He'd been on the treadmill at max incline—for two hours.

In an instant, I realized that I'd never worked that hard at anything. More importantly, I wasn't willing to either. To that point, I'd defaulted to an above-average baseline of talents and capabilities, but those only go so far. Natural talents have to be developed and crafted over many years, cared for and practiced with diligence and passion. They have to be put to the test. Eventually, hard work wins, but that day in Orlando, I knew I was starting to lose. I was losing my grip on my dreams. I was losing my grip on everything fascinating about the world in which I lived. And I was losing my grip on the life I wanted. I never became a physicist. I never became a mountaineer or worked in a profession that required me to be outdoors. I'd sit at a desk and look at spreadsheets for the next twenty years. I worked hard and saw some success but was never that passionate about anything I did. It was routine, boring, and hardly satisfying.

Fast forward many years. In the spring of 2018, I was working for a trade association for the Aerospace & Defense industry in Washington, DC. I was the Vice President for Membership, and one of my areas of responsibility was as director of a supply chain conference that hosted three large events per year with big industry integrators like Lockheed

Martin, Boeing, Northrop Grumman, and others. I was responsible for tailoring the agendas of each conference to relevant industry and supply chain issues, and once in a while, I'd mix things up and bring in a motivational speaker. It added a little energy and intrigue to the agenda, and the participants always enjoyed something a little more upbeat and different. Our next conference would be in Indianapolis, Indiana, with Rolls-Royce, one of the world's best aircraft engine manufacturers, and I thought of Jamie.

Oddly enough, it turned out that Jamie's speaking engagements were managed by Keppler Speakers, headquartered in Arlington, Virginia, just down the street from my office. I also played softball with their Vice President. As such, I was able to skip a few places in line and get Jamie booked for the conference. Although we'd never actually met—aside from getting his autograph after the conference at Disney twenty years earlier—I'd thought of Jamie often over the years and was excited to see him again. It was like seeing an old friend. This time it was more personal, and as the conference director, I'd arranged to meet with him one-on-one. Ten minutes before his presentation, I eagerly sought him out in a crowd of over three hundred people. In so many words, I told him about Disney, about the photograph, and I told him that he changed my life.

He took the stage and told the same stories I'd heard many years before. He was larger than life just like he was then, every bit as inspirational as he was before, and the fire in my heart was just as strong. And after he finished his last words— with a still applauding crowd and a tear rolling down the side of my face—he descended the stage and met me in the middle of that auditorium with the greatest bear hug of my life. I believe everyone there that day knew it was a moment for us both. In that embrace, I'd remember what he'd signed on that postcard twenty years earlier: "Hey Dan, climb on! – Jamie." A few things in my life had come full circle, and I knew what I needed to do next.

A month later, I'd resign from a very comfortable and high-profile job to pursue a pre-revenue start-up in the technology sector. I'd take a major risk at arguably the most important point in my career. My salary would be dependent on seed investors for next three years and hardly guaranteed. I'd fail hundreds of times to bring on new investors, and every dollar I did raise would hit my bank account a few days before my last paycheck ran out. But in doing so, I also found the time and energy to finally pursue my real passion—writing this book for you.

Over the course of writing this book, Jamie and I have become friends. I appreciate his wisdom and candor, and I've enjoyed the many conversations we've had over the final months of composing this book. Will I join him on his next expedition—an opportunity to once again follow him out that auditorium door, to a life of adventure and discovery? Perhaps.

As I was finishing up this manuscript, I also sent Mark a sample of this chapter. He is now the President and CEO of a successful government services business in Washington, DC, a firm he helped build since our days at PwC. He loved the story, and during that same exchange told me that his Chief Operating Officer had recently announced his retirement. He asked me if I'd be interested in the job. With the start-up at a critical go/no-go point (and at a point where my skills and efforts had met their logical conclusion), and in the best interest of my family and career, I agreed.

After a lengthy interview process, and as a truly dark horse candidate, Mark called to offer me the job on April 19, 2021. That same morning, I was on the phone with Jamie, catching up on the past few months—the intersection of destinies almost too much to explain in words. And as Jamie would say, "in an odd twist of fate" the bosses' kids from that boardroom twenty-two years ago would again reunite as CEO and COO.

How would things have been different, had I not chosen that exact seat at the boardroom table that day as an intern? It's just crazy to think about. But from this story—from this experience—I came to draw two simple conclusions, two lessons that form the cornerstone of any successful career or endeavor: Build good relationships and work hard, because eventually the combination of those two will win. Do those two things and life will generally work out the way it's supposed to. At a minimum, you'll have the assurance that you gave it your best shot with some really great people at your side—which should always be enough.

In the end, I believe Walter Bentley was trying to say that no matter what you bolt on, whether it be a turbo charger or any of the falsehoods we fill our lives with, nothing replaces a strong motor. At the heart of that motor is love. And with that, we'll all find happiness. We'll find meaningful relationships. We'll climb any mountain!

CHAPTER 17

THE PUZZLE

"There are no extra pieces in the universe. Everyone is here because he or she has a place to fill, and every piece must fit itself into the big jigsaw puzzle."

- Deepak Chopra

The living room at the lake house was oddly quiet. Not silent, just quieter than usual. Through a wall of floor-to-ceiling windows, nature bestowed her simple elegance. She showed her craft, her art form, and a variety of her wondrous brushstrokes vividly radiated across the dark surface below—a humid midsummer night breeze, a delicate glitter of moonlight, a playful dance of tiny ripples, and a gentle patting of small waves against her sandy shoreline. They were small gifts in themselves.

My family and I were spending the weekend together with some close friends and had just finished a long, hot day at Lake Anna, Virginia. My Aunt Barbie retired there a number of years ago, and we make a couple summer visits each year, oftentimes with other families and friends. A typical lake house dinner feast, probably enough calories to sustain the average human for several days, had now begun to drain whatever energy we had left. Our kids were watching a movie in another room, and my wife and I and another couple had assumed our final post of the day on the living room couches, heads and feet fully consumed by the overstuffed cushions and pillows. We were totally exhausted, stuffed, sun soaked, and temporarily suspended from the gravity of our daily lives—at momentary peace with the universe. But I couldn't help but notice the unusual softness of the scene. Something was very different.

Despite the magnificence of the moment, it felt somewhat incomplete. And then it dawned on me. It wasn't some "thing" that was missing, it was someone. My gregarious and immensely loving and generous Aunt Barbie was nowhere to be seen. She is certainly a character. She's larger than life, and we've shared more memories than I can possibly count or even remember. She's a wonderful person, very much a second mother to me and also a close friend, and I usually know it when she's not in the room. But where was she now? She certainly wasn't one to sit out a late-night laugh with friends and family. I'd eventually find her, and what followed would be an abrupt and unexpected shift in my general understanding of life itself.

A couple minutes later, I got up to use the bathroom and there she was, in a side room doing something most unusual— putting together a jigsaw puzzle. I've never seen my aunt sit still for more three seconds, much less have the attention and patience for a thousand-piece puzzle. It was an odd sight, not one that I'd seen before, and puzzles were certainly not an interest of hers, not one I knew about anyway. More peculiar than my aunt doing something so seemingly out of character was the almost immediate analogy it revealed to me about life—it's a puzzle with many, many, many pieces. It doesn't come with a legend or a neat picture on the front of the box of what it's supposed to look like in the end. It's a puzzle that, through our limited understanding, may appear to be missing a few pieces. And every puzzle is different, unique to the number of people who've ever lived.

According to Guinness World Records, the record for the jigsaw puzzle with the most pieces was set on September 24, 2011 at Pho Tho Stadium in Vietnam. Students from the University of Economics of Ho Chi Minh City—1,600 in total—assembled the 551,232-1piece puzzle in just over seventeen hours, more than doubling the previous record of 212,323 pieces. The finished puzzle, depicting a lotus flower and the words "One will. One dream. One Power." in both Vietnamese and English, would eventually measure 3,708 square feet, just over three quarters the size of an NBA basketball court.

Now those students didn't put that puzzle together because it was easy. A puzzle with that many pieces is designed to be hard. But piece by piece, they worked together and accomplished something great in the end. And if every minute of your life is a piece of the puzzle (and you live to the US median age of seventy-eight), you'll have put together a puzzle with 41,000,000 pieces—breaking the world record by more than seventy-four times. And just like those students, you'll have put together your puzzle with the help of thousands of people and countless experiences, legends of a different sort. But the trick is, it's not an easy thing to do. We all need someone to show us the way. We all need help. And if life doesn't come with a picture on the front of the box—a key—then how do we know how to put our puzzles together? How do we see the bigger picture?

Perhaps we do need a legend. Maybe—better said—we need legends. We need a collection of small pieces, small experiences, that eventually form a larger whole. At first, the pieces have straight edges and corners, and they form the boundaries of the possible. They frame our morality and ethics and, most importantly, our character. Then the inner pieces form small patterns, areas of similar color and texture—perhaps the people we surround ourselves with. Eventually images start to emerge, guideposts. And while the task can be frustrating, while we may fail to put certain pieces together correctly the first time, we keep trying, and eventually we start to build who we are. We start to get hints at the bigger picture. We gain clarity and energy and confidence, and eventually we get it. And despite how daunting or scary the journey seemed at the beginning, we finally recognize our role in the great machine.

In my very humble opinion, there are only a few absolute truths in life. There are very few things that humans are designed to empirically know. There are so many unanswered questions—big, complex, infinitely regressed (for example, if God created the universe, who created God?), and oftentimes confusing questions. Many times, life can be quite scary. It's dangerous. It's full of uncertainty and death. It's not fair. And too often it might seem like there's only darkness at the end of the tunnel. But this isn't necessarily bad news. These things keep life mysterious. They keep our attention on continuing to put the puzzle together. They preserve the excitement and beauty of discovery. They preserve faith. They teach us the importance and purity of true love. And they give us a sense of urgency, because we're not guaranteed anything, and no one else is responsible for putting our own puzzles together. It's difficult for me to imagine how life could be any other way.

To me, life is a patchwork of small discoveries, ones that eventually weave an intricate tapestry of faith and experience. They give us just enough knowledge and hope to persist and persevere, even during the most challenging of life's trials. They provide the mechanism of meaning, how we make sense out of our lives and this crazy universe we find ourselves in.

I believe we're tasked with putting our own puzzles together, the individual pieces being our experiences and the information and people we choose to interact with day to day. Each piece—by itself usually quite ordinary—is necessary to tell the whole story, which is our experience of the world, beginning to end. And just like those students in Vietnam, we all need help; to do something great and to show us the way. I've been shown the way by countless people and thousands of small experiences in my life. They are the pieces of my puzzle. And by that definition, we're all legends. But I don't believe any pieces are missing. I believe I've always had what I needed to fulfill my ultimate purpose, which is the embodiment and expression of love and our connections with other people— ultimately returning to a purer state.

I don't believe God or the universe wasted any energy with pieces that didn't fit into the larger whole; the greatest example being the law of conservation of energy—that energy is neither created or lost, only converted from one form to another. That conversion in its most basic sense—the energy we expel in our daily lives—is how we react and ultimately view the things that happen to us. We can choose to spend that energy for good or not. And if we're given the freedom of choice, should the puzzle ever be a mystery? Maybe all we ever needed was that choice? Choices, ultimately, put the puzzle together for us. They're the basis of our experience. Again, this is not as easy for some people as it is for others, but it is our reality (from what we can tell anyway). A major choice, though, is where we choose to look.

If I took a closer look at my Aunt Barbie's puzzle that day, I'm sure there would have been a few pieces that looked like me and my family. The piece that looks like her—a big piece—is certainly in mine.

CHAPTER 18

THE DRUM

"I played my drum for him.... I played my best for him.... Then he smiled at me. Me and my drum."

*- Bob Seger and the Silver Bullet
Band, Little Drummer Boy*

Not all drums are the same. They come in all different shapes and sizes. They make different noises. Some are big. Some are small. Some are new. Some are old. Some last a long time, others break quickly out of the box. When drums break, sometimes we can fix them; other times we cannot. But while we have our drum, we should be grateful that we have an instrument to play, that the music we create can be a light for others. And regardless of which drum we get, our responsibility is always the same—to play it the best we can.

On December 8, 2019, I gave the following Christmas sermon at a church in Northern Virginia. Many family members and friends were in attendance that day, and it was one of the greatest experiences of my life.

Good afternoon. My name is Danny Olmes.
I hope everyone's having a good start to their holiday season, and I assume, while sometimes stressful, Christmastime is most everyone's favorite time of year. Today I was asked to speak about John the Baptist and preparing the way of the Lord.

This message is even more meaningful to our family, as next weekend, our two children, Chase and Berkeley, will be baptized. I want them to know that I'm prouder of them than they will ever know. The experience of being your father is not one that I can adequately describe with words. I've read a lot of things on religion and spirituality, and there's a word that often comes up in those texts to describe spiritual or mystical experiences. The word is "ineffable." Being your father, the love I have for you, is ineffable. You are the most precious gift of my life, and I love you both more than anything.

I think most Christians know John the Baptist as the man who baptized Jesus—the man who stood on the banks of the river Jordan, somewhat confused as to why the sinless Messiah would ask to be baptized. Jesus tells him, "Let it be so now; it is proper for us to do this to fulfill all righteousness." (Matthew 3:15)

Honestly, that's kind of a vague answer and one that is certainly open to interpretation. I had to ask myself what "to fulfill all righteousness" meant. And how is that "preparing the way of the Lord?" Especially at Christmastime.

Christmastime is a time of year that feels different and certainly brings out the best in most of us. It's a time of cherished memories, great stories and movies, the company of friends and loved ones. It's a time that just feels a bit more peaceful. A calmer state that we spend the rest of the year seeking.

There's a special place in my heart for those whom that's not the case. For those that are alone. For our brothers and sisters who are lost and for those who've grown weary while searching for their place in the world.

There's a wonderful scene in the movie The Last Jedi. Luke Skywalker and Rey, his young Jedi apprentice, are conversing in a temple cave on Luke's private island where he has decided to live out his days as a hermit. Luke is lamenting on his failure as a Jedi master, specifically his failure to keep the young Kylo Ren from being seduced by the dark side. In the ominous shadows of a setting sun pouring in through an opening in the cave, he tells Rey that he was the legend that never actually was. And Rey says to him, "Well, the galaxy may need a legend...I need someone to show me my place in all this." As a Jedi herself (the Jedi being the most powerful and spiritually connected entities in the galaxy) she's still unsure of her greater purpose. She's asking to be shown the way.

My friends, I think this story represents a pretty clear analogy to all of us. Aren't we all seeking to understand our place in the world? That's not an easy thing to do. We all need someone to show us the way. In other words…we all need a legend.

Standing there with John the Baptist, and perhaps long before that, Jesus had to decide: Am I going to be merely a man, or am I going to be history's greatest teacher? Am I going to be the leader of leaders? Am I going to be the Savior of the human race?

We all know what his decision ultimately was, and from that point forward, Jesus would preach forgiveness and love to the multitudes. He would heal the sick and perform many miracles. He would conquer death and inspire billions. And his words would echo loudly across the next 2,000 years.

In his dying days, Napoleon—himself one of history's greatest leaders—would say this of Jesus:

"I know men, and I tell you that Jesus Christ is no mere man. Between Him and every other person in the world there is no possible term of comparison. Alexander, Caesar, Charlemagne, and I have founded empires. But on what did we rest the creation of our genius? Upon force. Jesus Christ founded His empire upon love; and at this hour…millions of men would die for Him."

He goes on to say: "From the first day to the last He is the same; majestic and simple; infinitely firm and infinitely gentle. He proposes a series of mysteries and commands with authority that we should believe them…giving no other reason than those tremendous words, 'I am God.'"

Those mysteries and commands, brothers and sisters, are the greatest gifts we've been given. They are the fulfillment of righ-

teousness. Life itself, freedom, the gifts of love, compassion, and forgiveness. The confirmation that we're all spiritual beings. The promise that our experience in mortality is not in vain, and the promise of eternity.

Once upon a time, I criticized these things, and I've also stood at the river. But I haven't always stood there with a clear conscience. I haven't always stood there as the man I wanted to be. It's not been easy, but I've come to understand that the question I need to answer every day, and regardless of what happened yesterday, is am I going to follow him or not? Am I preparing myself for eternity or am I not?

In fulfilling all righteousness, in preparing the way of the Lord, Jesus made possible a simple choice—the choice to be like him. Our Father's hope for us is that we find peace in that choice and that we find happiness on that journey home. That amidst the uncertainty and the bad things that happen, our faith didn't waver. That we gave this thing called life our best shot and that maybe we learned a few things along the way. To me, it's that simple. We confuse the simplicity because sometimes we forget who we truly are—the sons and daughters of the divine.

I'm reading a book by Aldous Huxley called, The Perennial Philosophy. In it he writes: "It's because we don't know Who we are, because we are unaware that the Kingdom of Heaven is within us, that we behave in the generally silly, the often insane, the sometimes criminal ways that are so characteristically human. We are saved, liberated, and enlightened by perceiving the unper-

ceived good that is already within us, by returning to our eternal Ground and remaining where, without knowing it, we've always been."

He continues: "It's only by becoming Godlike that we can know God—and to become Godlike is to identify ourselves with the divine element which in fact, constitutes our essential nature, but of which in our mainly voluntary ignorance we choose to remain unaware."

And as Jesus told us at the Last Supper: "If you love me, keep my commands. And I will ask the Father, and he will give you another advocate to help you and be with you forever—the Spirit of truth. The world cannot accept him, because it neither sees him nor knows him. But you know him, for he lives with you and will be in you. I will not leave you as orphans; I will come to you. Before long, the world will not see me again, but you'll see me. Because I live, you also will live. On that day you'll realize that I am in my Father, and you are in me, and I am in you."

This holiday season, I'm reminded that the greatest gift I can give is to commit myself to something higher—to an eternal standard—and to the simple words of Jesus Christ: "Follow me." One of my friends here today, Tom Seneca, said recently that the greatest gift we can give our children is the knowledge of and commitment to a life of faith. I want you to know Tom, that I wrote that down in a little journal I keep, and so long as I'm alive, I'll remember what you said.

Brothers and sisters, I'd like to leave you with my commitment to Jesus Christ through my favorite Christmas story which is told in the song "Little Drummer Boy."

Upon hearing the news of the newborn King, a little boy comes running, but he quickly realizes something. He says, little baby, I'm a poor boy too. I don't have anything to give you Lord, but I've got this little drum. Can I play it for you? And then the little boy said, "I played my drum for him. And I played my best for him." Then he smiled at me. Me and my drum.

My friends, the greatest gift we can give, the mission we're sent here to accomplish is to wake up every morning and play our drum and play it the best we can.

Playing my drum means being Christ-like. Being well-intentioned and honest. Being kind and compassionate. Being likable and lighthearted. Being an observer and a good listener, and standing up for what's right. Playing my drum is always a choice—a choice I can make regardless of anything else. And it's the faith in our legend, Jesus Christ, and our full effort that puts a smile on that little baby's face—a smile that leads us home.

Merry Christmas everyone. I leave this with you in the name of Jesus Christ.

Amen.

Just keep playing your drum. Play it as long as you can, and play it loud!

CHAPTER 19

THE SHORT SHORTS

"He who desires to see the living God face-to-face should not seek him in the empty, firmament of his mind, but in human love."

- Fyodor Dostoevsky

O kay, so the title of this chapter might be a little misleading, but I can't help but start it off with a funny anecdote before I dive into some of the most important encounters of my life. This chapter is not about booty shorts, though I admit—when I run—I wear very short shorts, and to echo the urban poets of the early 1990s, *"There's no shame in my game."* Without a doubt, they're the most comfortable and functional clothing for the job, but aside from running, they shouldn't be worn in public, certainly not by a middle-aged man with any consideration for the general welfare of others. A set of pale, hairy legs is probably on most people's "Top 10 Things I Never Want To See Again" list—a list, of course, that's reserved for those with the terrible bad luck of seeing them the first time. These shorts are the Daisy Dukes of my generation, and they were standard issue for NBA basketball players until the mid-90s when the emergence of hip-hop music finally normalized the apparel of American athletes. Repeat after me: "Thank you, Dr. Dre! Rest in peace, B.I.G."

My wife is embarrassed by my choices, but I love every minute of it. I have to admit there's a deep satisfaction when my neighbors ask, "Have you seen that guy in the neighborhood running with no clothes on?" and her answer is, painfully, "Yes. That's my husband." My favorite pair of short shorts has an American flag pattern across the front and back and is so short that without the swim trunk mesh on the inside, "stuff" would literally be flying everywhere. And my favorite outfit is nothing—shirtless—bringing only my American flag shorts, bird chest, and black bandanna and sunglasses to "bare." It's as close to streaking as the authorities can tolerate before it becomes an issue of public indecency, and if you saw me from a distance—without knowing me personally—your first thought would likely be, "OMG. What a douchebag!" But I promise, when you get to know me, I'm actually a cool dude.

Occasionally, I'll make an unexpected pass as my wife is out talking with our neighbors. I can see the look on her face, her eyes rolling and straining as she futilely resists the magnificence of my angelic gait. I can see her posture, her body slightly cocked to the side—at an angle—as she tries, hopelessly, to distance herself from the unfolding greatness. I see a hand above her brow, head down, avoiding eye contact and certain public humiliation. "That's my husband!" These words should be carved in granite and put in a high place for all to see. Of course, she could lie, but the level of contempt and disappointment she must be feeling in this moment would be hard to fake, and I take great pleasure in her momentary misfortune. My wife's friends, and even some of the mothers on my son's baseball team, say that I have better legs than most women, a compliment that any alpha male would quickly sweep under the never-to-be-acknowledged-again rug. To my wife, these are low moments, and I love every one of them. They are the only defense I have left. But I digress.

And although my friends and neighbors have seen more of my skinny, white ass than they probably care to, the following pages are a not a tribute to my running wardrobe or to the folklore of a half-naked suburban warrior. They're a collection of even shorter stories, and they are perhaps my most powerful. They're a testament to some of my basic understandings of life itself that I've learned from the most unexpected of events and people—those that we all share.

THE LIEUTENANT

I'm not a fan of bumper stickers. I tend to reserve my political viewpoints and sarcasm for a lucky few, and I don't like to brag about my honor roll student. But not too long ago, I was out running an errand at Target when I saw the greatest bumper sticker of my life. To say it was profound would be an understatement. I hadn't heard it before, but it's actually pretty popular. It reads, "If you can't stand behind our troops, stand in front of them." The saying hit me square in the heart. It's a powerful statement and a basic challenge. It's simple yet so complex, and it probably means different things to different people.

I've always loved and appreciated our brave men and women in uniform. I almost became one of them. Looking back, I wish I had. But perhaps I don't think about them enough, and maybe it shouldn't take a bumper sticker to occasionally remind me of what it means to be an American. In particular, I have a strong love and admiration for the men and women of our enlisted ranks—our young sons and daughters who stand at the front line ready to defend us at a moment's notice. And they get paid next to nothing to do it.

There's an unfortunate disparity in the world—that those who volunteer to defend our freedom are the ones who have, by comparison, so little of it. They come from cities and towns across America where oftentimes a college education and a six-figure salary exist only in the realms of fantasy—they're not accessible realities. They risk their lives to preserve our way of life, a way of life they might never see. And we should know something is off when the CEO of the company who sells the tank makes five hundred times more than the person driving it. We owe them more.

This random trip to Target would help frame an experience I'd had many years earlier with one of our country's unknown heroes. He was the Second Lieutenant who hung the finishing medal around my neck at my second Marine Corps Marathon in Washington, DC. When the gun fired that day, I thought I was running the race to accomplish something great, and perhaps I did. The physical exhaustion and perseverance I felt in that moment were memorable, and maybe more so was my pride at the finality of the finish line. After months of dedication and training, I'd achieved my goal—a sub-four-hour marathon. But that feeling would prove inferior to the life-changing perspective I immediately gained just seconds later.

As I crossed the finish line, I walked a few paces ahead to receive my medal. As I made my approach, time seemed to slow, as if the moment would reveal something special, and as I crept through a pack of sweaty, exhausted runners, I finally arrived at my final destination of the day—a clean-shaven young man with a nice-looking ribbon and medal. To be honest, this moment made me feel a bit awkward; it was an honor I somehow didn't deserve. Adorned from head to toe in his fatigues, the young Marine hung the medal on my neck, shook my hand, and with the most sincere voice and expression said, "Thank you, sir. Congratulations!"

Twenty-four hours a day and 365 days a year, this young man defends my freedom, and for a brief moment in time, he thanks *me* for voluntarily running an unnecessary distance. I looked him in the eye, and the only thing I could think to say was, "No, sir. Thank you!"

THE DRIVER

Every morning, thousands of people pass through the turn-stiles at the train station in Reston, Virginia, most of them on their daily commute from Northern Virginia into our nation's capital. The platform is a concrete Goliath and a sea of unfamiliar faces: men, women, children, the youthful, the aged, the happy, the sad, the rich, the poor, and everyone in between. Personally, I love taking the train. I love to watch people do what they do, and there's no better people watching than on public transportation. I've walked these platforms hundreds of times in my commute to work, but one morning stood out more than the rest. It would change everything. And oddly enough, the whisper of this experience—the true secret—only revealed itself years later as I began to write this story and reflect on its true meaning. And it required that I look at an otherwise ordinary experience in an extraordinary way.

If you're like me, the last thing you want when you're determined to get somewhere is to be slowed down—to be bothered. No one likes standing in line, sitting in traffic, or being in an otherwise awkward or boring conversation that offers little hope of escape. On my morning commute, my goal is usually pretty singular—get from here to there as quickly and with as little interruption as possible. I'm not necessarily in a rush. As I said, the people watching, and the experience of the shuffle, is fascinating to me. But I want the transition from here to there to be on my terms. I don't like being interrupted. Perhaps it's because this is the only time I really have to myself, and it's a precious time. But on a random winter morning, one interruption was most necessary, and it proved to be life-altering.

As I approached the turnstiles that morning in my tan wool overcoat, black beanie, and Bose studio headphones (and probably with a confident strut in my To Boot New York dress shoes), I started to get a sense that someone was watching me. I felt a subtle pull from somewhere, a feeling that someone's eyes were focused on me a little longer than they should have. Something ahead of me wasn't right, and I started to feel the world close in around me as I became the quick target of a stranger's attention.

We've all had the sensation of being watched. It can be unnerving. There's just something about it, the primal suspicion and the feeling of being hunted. And before I could fully process what was happening, an older gentleman quickly approached me and said, "Man, you lookin' sharp today, brotha. You remind of JFK Jr! You gots to be a Kennedy!" Thought bubbles were popping everywhere inside my head:

"Huh?" "WTF are you talking about?" "Who are you?" "Seriously WTF is going on?"

I was completely bewildered. Naturally, I began to size him up from head to toe. Who was this person? What did he want from me? And, most importantly, was he a threat? I glanced up and down at him as I gathered more information, and at first pass, it was immediately clear from his uniform and the various gadgets on his hip belt that he was a Metro security guard. But more curious, though, was his demeanor, the way he looked at me, and his smile. He almost seemed starstruck, like I was some kind of celebrity, and I could feel his energy and passion, the same feeling you'd have when reuniting with an old friend. But why me? Out of the thousands of people in the train station that morning, what was so special about me? So, I began to go through a long list of assumptions, but ego sort of took over, and I initially just assumed he was a friendly guy simply paying me a compliment. Maybe he noticed a little jive in my step, an edge, and he wanted to give some props to this suburban white boy. So, I said, "Thank you" and tried to be polite and move on, but he seemed intent on keeping my attention, moving in front of me until I was cornered. But regardless of the momentary stroking of my ego and the strong desire to continue on with my day, deep down I knew what was happening. His body language and energy and persistence revealed his intent. He was trying to tell me a story.

So, I loosened my jaw and took a time-out from everything else. In the meantime, two trains would leave on the platform below, nonetheless, I gave him my full attention; and for the next five minutes, he told me about his time as a driver for the Kennedy family in Massachusetts and about his personal relationship with John F. Kennedy Jr. With every sentence—every memory—it became clearer to me just how proud he was of that part of his life and how much it meant to him—a little-known prestige and an internal confirmation that he mattered. I believe he sought me out that morning so he could tell his story and relive a part of his life that brought him great joy. Maybe he didn't have people in his life that he could share that story with or anyone who saw past his color, his age, and the cheap metal badge on his uniform. That morning was never about me. I gave him a gift that he probably needed for a very long time—I just listened.

THE ADAMS FAMILY

Sometimes we just don't know how good we've got it. From time to time, we need a reminder, a wakeup call, or maybe a punch in the mouth, that perhaps our daily annoyances— our "first world problems" as so many like to say—should be placed in a little box called "Perspective." Or "Gratitude."

One morning not too long ago, I was getting my two kids ready for a short trip to do some volunteer work at the ADAMS Center in Herndon, Virginia. ADAMS stands for the All Dulles Area Muslim Society, and their mission is "To provide religious, social, and educational services to enable the Muslim community to fulfill its responsibilities and contribute to the betterment of society by embodying and exemplifying leadership and excellence and fostering peace." They were the nicest people I've ever met, and that morning they were sponsoring a coat and blanket drive for Syrian refugees.

My kids complained for thirty minutes. They couldn't be bothered. They wanted to watch some annoying YouTuber, play Fortnite, run around outside, or do nothing at all. They wanted to be lazy. Perhaps they didn't really understand what we were going to do and why it was important. Maybe I should've given them the benefit of the doubt, but I sort of snapped. I got right in their faces. Intense. Eye-to-eye. I wanted them to remember what I was about to say. "Sit down!" I said. "I'm going to show you who we're going to help! I want you to know, right now, how some people live. I want you to know, right now, just how lucky you really are!"

For the next five minutes, I showed them pictures of the Syrians refugees—in particular pictures of children—just like them. I showed them the horror of the refugee camps, the endless rows of dirty tents, the burning trash, the destroyed cities, the bloodshed, the wailing of innocent people of all ages, and the hopelessness—all things that don't exist in our neighborhood. It wasn't easy. It was clear they were seeing something they'd never seen before, something they didn't know existed at all, and it was a lot for two nine-year-olds to process. But they got it.

I didn't say another word, and I didn't hear another complaint. For the entire twenty-minute ride to the ADAMS Center, they sat in total silence as they each stared out their windows. They were shocked, somber, slightly ashamed of their ignorance, grateful, and, most importantly, ready to help. Mission accomplished.

THE GENTLEMAN BARISTA

I can't even remember why I had a suit on, but it was my best suit. It was neatly pressed and it fit perfectly. Beneath the fabric was a very good version of me. I was in great shape, and I felt better spiritually and emotionally than I had in a long time—maybe ever.

On a day like any other, I was in line at a local coffee shop waiting for my turn to order. In my usual and proper form as an observer, I was calmly scanning the room, watching the comings and goings of the shop patrons. Mostly unaware of my musings, I watched them as they did the things people do in a coffee shop: hypnotically staring at smartphones, feverishly clicking keys on laptops, posturing at the cream and sugar stand, and isolating themselves behind noise-cancelling headphones.

When I finally approached the young man behind the cash register, I smiled, gave him a typical head nod, and said,

"What's up man!" Behind a curtain of dreadlocks, he appeared almost dazed. He didn't really respond at first, and then I felt the scene shift a bit. There was a slight pause as his eyes clicked back and forth across my suit jacket and necktie. And with a curious, but confident grin, he said: "That suit looks really clean, my man! Someday I'm gonna' look like you!"

Everything around me, the hustle and bustle and the clicking and clacking of the coffee shop, came to a noticeable halt—a momentary silence. All the usual inputs were temporarily, and perhaps purposefully, muted, and I was pulled into this unique moment, totally engrossed in the facial expressions of this young man in front of me. He wore a subtle but confident smirk, and his head shook and bobbed just slightly, affirming what I believe was a vision he had for the future. I saw the pride in his eyes, one of intense personal optimism. I saw a newfound confidence as his imagination ran wild, creating an image of his future self—his best self. And I saw hope. It was beautiful.

I ordered my coffee, left the store, and I never saw him again. But I walked away floating. I was a very good version of me that day, inside and out. Perhaps he recognized that over everything else and saw a mirror image of his himself. Maybe one day this young man will become the CEO of a Fortune 500 company. Maybe he'll start his own business and see great success. Or maybe, he'll become an ordinary guy like me, a gentleman poised to change someone's life with a suit.

Some people say that beauty is only skin deep. Others say that image is everything. And you know what? They're both right. You don't have to be beautiful, but how you look matters, inside and out.

THE PINK PANTHER

For whatever reason, I was having a bad day. I had a shitty attitude, and my energy level was one notch from the bottom. My shoulders felt heavy, my eyes sticky, my head was in a slight fog, and it seemed like a workout just to keep my body upright from the waist. I probably didn't get enough sleep the night before and likely went to bed full of junk food, which is the usual combination that leads to what I was feeling that morning.

I got off the train and weaved my way through downtown Rosslyn, Virginia, just across the river from Washington, DC. After a short walk, I entered the lobby of my office building and began the final trek through a large indoor terrace with snaking escalators, a few small shops, and lots of high windows with light pouring through them. It's a passageway that's usually full of people, most coming from the main street and heading to a bank of elevators to lift them to their final destinations. The lobby is also wide, and people tend to keep their distance, avoiding eye contact and awkward exchanges. I always found the lack of interaction or acknowledgement from the people passing by to be somewhat isolating. But it was also peaceful, this huge space with a life of its own: a huge "living wall" of plants and flowers, a subtle indoor breeze, rays of early morning light shining through the windows, and the mild echoing of hard-soled dress shoes against the tiled floor. I always looked forward to that walk and those last few minutes to collect my thoughts before they'd no longer be mine for the next nine hours, before the grind of an average workday.

That morning I had on a pair of flat-front khaki dress pants and a neatly pressed pink dress shirt. The outfit fit well, and I thought it was an appropriate choice for an early summer day. Looking back, I may never have had this experience had I not chosen that exact outfit on that exact day. I was looking sharp that morning, and to the rest of the world, I probably looked pretty tip-top. Even so, I still felt like shit, but not for long.

As I stepped into the elevator and hit the button for floor seventeen, I heard a thundering presence approaching, and before I knew what was happening, a three-hundred-pound tsunami of jewelry, fingernails, and hair extensions poured into the elevator with me. I was hit with a determined wave of sight and sound, and also smell. Her perfume was so intense, it almost made me sneeze. The best part was this woman's body language. She was big and beautiful and didn't give a shit who knew it. She took one look at me and said, "Oh damn, sugar…. You lookin' fine today boy! Mmmmm, mmmmm. I love that shirt, sweetie."

More thought bubbles inside my head: *"Oh shit.... She just hit the button for floor twenty!"* *"This person could eat me alive, in more ways than one!"* *"WTF do I say?"* *"She's so confident!"* *"This is awkward, but I love it!"* *"What's happening here?"* *"I'm going to pee my pants!"*

I politely said, "Thank you," as I didn't know how to properly articulate a compliment in return, certainly not in the five-second elevator ride to the seventeenth floor. The handbags, the endless accessories, the feeling of being totally-eye raped by this animal on the prowl, and the wilderness of glistening ebony curls caused a sensory overload, a momentary short circuit in my hopelessly unprepared brain. It was like a glitch in *The Matrix*. And if Keanu Reeves had been there, he would've agreed and probably would've repeated his now-famous line from the movie: *"Whoa!"*

As I exited the elevator I said, "Bye now," and with a naughty grin, this woman in her late forties said, "Bye." I stepped into the landing area of my office and curiously looked back. Through a set of closing elevator doors, I saw the most intense "fuck-me eyes" I'd ever seen in my life. The only thing that would've revealed her intentions more would be if she was licking her full, glossy lips from one side to the other. The doors slammed together, and I never saw her again. All I could do was smile. I chuckled to myself and shook my head slightly to acknowledge the craziness of what had just happened.

What a compliment, and what an outrageous experience, so unexpected and so perfectly human. It completely changed my day. In fact, it changed my month. It was a much-needed shot in the arm and a reminder of something very basic. What I learned in that moment was the power of a simple compliment. It's not hard. It doesn't take much time. And it can be as simple as saying, "I like your shirt."

Say something nice to someone. It could change their day. In my case, it changed thirty of them. I thought about the experience off and on for a month, and every time, it brought a smile to my face.

THE FEAST

It was about 9:30 a.m., and I had just finished up a business breakfast with a colleague at a local restaurant. I said my goodbyes and headed to the bathroom—one last pit stop before I began my day. As is the case in most restaurants, the bathrooms were situated behind the bar and down a short, dark corridor. I did my thing and as I walked back toward the bar to leave, I noticed something a bit unusual. There was a gentleman sitting alone at the bar. In front of him was the most elaborate feast I'd ever seen. As I walked closer, I started to inventory the event: steak, eggs, pancakes, sausage, bacon, toast, a bowl of fruit, a bowl of grits, orange juice, and a cup of coffee. It was a ton of food, and he was clearly a reservation of one. Everything was aligned to a T, including his hard hat to the right and his work gloves to the left.

As I walked by, things seem to slow down, and I paused to watch as he savored every bite. It didn't take me long to add up what that breakfast feast probably cost. With tip, it could've easily been fifty bucks, an expensive breakfast for sure. It also didn't take me long to do the math. Obviously, a fifty-dollar breakfast for this man was a little different than a fifty-dollar breakfast for me, and I looked at the feast as a percentage of our incomes. Needless to say, it would be a lot more for me—maybe ten times more. The first question that came to mind was, "How often do I have $500 breakfast?" The second was how much I would enjoy it if I did. The first answer was, "never." And the second answer was…well, let's just say, I didn't like the second answer. I still have a lot of work to do. I probably take far too many things in my life for granted.

THE BODYGUARDS

They were two guys you didn't want to fuck with. If you got on their bad side, they'd tear you in half and not think twice. They might even do it because you're white, out of frustration and spite alone. And they just might do it for fun. But one day they came to my aid—they had my back—and I've never felt more comfortable with anyone. They were my protectors, and I'll be forever grateful they were with me that night. They stood at my side, and for just a few minutes, I felt like the king of the world.

Milton and Terry were two guys on my high school basketball team. I knew them both pretty well, as we'd been in school together since the seventh grade. And even though they were fifteen years old at the time, they were men among boys—a head taller, a hundred pounds heavier, and with muscles I didn't even know people had. They had square jaws and sharp facial features and not an ounce of fat on their bodies. Their hands and knuckles told a rough and solemn tale, marked by the scars of a type of warfare, a rough experience that was a world away from mine: an unfortunate standard of poverty and common street violence that affects too many. But they had big hearts. They were loyal to each other and to a select few, and they were my bodyguards one scary winter night.

I love basketball, in particular pick-up games—the physicality, the on-court rhythm and camaraderie of a team, the quickness of the game, and there's probably no better workout, honestly. Unfortunately, my skills developed more as a young adult. I was an athletic kid, but I was extremely undersized—almost frail. And as such, I was a little uncoordinated next to my peers who outweighed me by a hundred pounds or more. But as skinny as I was, I still had a bit of an attitude—a chip on my shoulder—and I loved talking trash. I loved the scuffle, competing, both physically and mentally, and I was a bit of a junkyard dog. I could bark through the fence all day long, but that was about it, and if the gate was ever opened, so to speak, I might be in trouble. One winter night, the gate got kicked in, and I was in *big* trouble.

It was a pretty standard old-school gymnasium: creaky wood floors and rickety bleachers, the smell of old sweat and mold, a grey dust ball blowing from here to there, and white concrete walls with several layers of cheap paint and scattered memories. Championship banners hung to honor years past and the forgotten successes of athletes long gone. Large fluorescent canister lights hung from the ceiling across a ribbon of steel rafters, each wrapped in a snaking bracelet of cords and electrical wires. The lights resembled little rocket engines, and they were about to cast an ominous shadow on the overconfidence of a skinny white kid. And they were also about to shine their light on one of the most important lessons of my life.

I finally got into the game late in the fourth quarter. We were leading by a decent margin, and it was time to clear the bench and get some playing time for the lower third of the roster, which included me. I checked myself into the game and found my opponent. He had a bushy afro and was stacked top to bottom with muscle. He was shorter than me but twice as fast. It was also immediately clear that this person didn't like me—his eyes burned with an attitude and hatred I hadn't seen before. I felt an apathy and indifference for my well-being from him, and it hit me right in the gut. I was a little scared, but I was mostly pissed. I didn't like this person because he didn't like me, and I made that immediately clear in the way I looked back at him. With my eyes, I said, "I can play this game, too, asshole. Fuck you!" I wanted to ruffle his feathers a bit, to get under his skin. Maybe it was a bit reckless—unnecessary. In the grand scheme of things, it made no difference at all. It wasn't going to affect the outcome of the game. It was simply an individual showdown on the world's most basic stage—the battlefield of an average basketball court.

No more than thirty seconds into the final two minutes of the game, I fouled him hard on a lay-up attempt. Tempers flared and he immediately came at me, ready to throw down. A small scuffle ensued, but like most on-court skirmishes it was quickly broken up by teammates. We walked our separate ways, each backpedaling and talking a little shit along the way. I'd spend the remaining minute and a half on our side of the court as our point guard wound down the clock. The final seconds ticked away, and the game was over. The initial battle had concluded, but the war had just begun. I knew that I'd face him one more time, and possibly a third, if he was lurking somewhere after the game, in the dark corridors of the school's hallways or parking lot—two frontiers I'd have to eventually cross to reach the safety of our team bus on the other side.

We lined up to shake hands, and I saw him three players back. I tapped the first two opponent's hands with the standard high five, and then we squared up, toe-to-toe. He came at me again, only this time, he was really ready to fight. It felt like rage. Again, the skirmish was broken up, but he said the one thing that scared me most: "I'll be wait'n for you, punk." The gate to the junkyard I referred to earlier just got slammed open. Terrified, I made my way past the benches and headed to the locker room. What I didn't realize during and after the game was that I had also pissed off a couple people in the crowd. When I glanced over at the stands, I saw three or four other students who were equally enraged, equally intent on my destruction. Looking back, it was a moment of profound isolation, vulnerability, and just primal fear. I was in danger, and I knew it.

I took a shower, put my borrowed tie and baggy jeans back on, and proceeded to pace around the locker room. When it came time to leave, I was still seated on one of the benches with my head down, my hands nervously clenched between my legs, and my right leg uncontrollably bouncing off the wet tile floor. I was genuinely scared, more than I'd been in my whole life. Leaving the protection of the visitor's locker room was not something I wanted to do, nor did I know what was waiting for me outside its walls, possibly an episode of violence I just wasn't ready for. And then two pairs of high tops appeared below my trembling hands. I looked up, and there they were. Milton and Terry. Terry only said seven words, but they brought me more comfort than any in my entire life. He said, "Come on, brotha. We got your back!"

So, with two of the baddest motherfuckers you've ever seen on my right and left, I was escorted out of that locker room, through a dark parking lot, and to the ultimate serenity of our school bus for the ride home. The looks Milton and Terry gave the crowd and the opposing players were straight out of a movie. I remember it like it was yesterday, and the best I can describe is this: "We'll fucking kill you if you come anywhere near our boy!" And no one did. No one dared.

In life, we sometimes talk of saviors, those that deliver us from evil and certain annihilation. They protect us, they take us to a promised land, and they lend a hand when we're most in need, oftentimes at our most vulnerable points. Milton and Terry were two of my saviors. They came to me in my most desperate hour and were ready for World War III on my behalf. I am grateful beyond words, and I love them like brothers. I hope this story reaches them one day.

A fight at a high school basketball game is not uncommon, but I learned a very uncommon lesson that day. Milton and Terry were from a world away. They didn't look like me. We shared almost nothing in common, and the disparity of our economics was as staggering as it was disheartening. But we shared this moment. We shared an uncommon bond, and it was a moment that transcended all the bullshit we see in the world—all the division, all the hate, and all the anger. "Come on, brotha. We got your back."

We can *all* have each other's backs. We can be so much better.

CHAPTER 20

THE REALLY SHORT SHORTS

Since everything is a reflection of our minds,
everything can be changed by our minds."

– Gautama Buddha

Okay. So I'm not still talking about my running shorts. But if I were, I'd say there's only one thing that's shorter. It's called a banana hammock, or to use a more conventional and universally understood term, a Speedo. If you don't know what a Speedo is, one, good for you, and two, let's just say it's a thin layer of fabric that's designed to conceal only the essential parts—principally the shaft, jewels, and balloon knot—with the least amount of material possible. It's an article of clothing that, outside of a competitive swimming event, no man should wear—not ever. And for the second time, I digress. You're welcome!

As I near the end of my story, I'd like to put forward some of my most memorable thoughts and observations; when we just take pause, when we listen, when we take a look around, the most beautiful things tend to reveal themselves in plain sight. Perhaps more appropriately termed, these are my reflections on the simple, common, and powerful experiences in my walk from here to there—on the journey that we all share. But I won't say it's easy.

What's easy is to get caught up in the endless and perceived torment of everyday life, only to miss the incredible beauty that's right in front of us—the beauty we spend a lifetime uncovering every last stone to find. The trick—I believe—is to notice the stones that are already turned over. Sometimes they're hard to find and sometimes they might not be what we think, but they're everywhere, and they truly are reflections— the mirror images of the Divine in all of us. Most of the time, we want the "booming voice from the sky," a direct answer to all of life mysteries, but I ask—and I challenge—why we can't hear that same message in the quiet whisperings of our daily lives, in the small stones that are already turned over. I also ask myself the questions: If all I ever heard was the booming voice, if I always had a loud answer to my questions and a painless resolution to all my problems, how I could I ever possibly live? And what would I ever actually learn? If I had to guess, I'd begin to resent the loud voice. I'd not-so-politely ask it to stop telling me what to do. I'd tell it I wanted to live my own life and figure it out on my own. Sound familiar? And yes, I assume you see the irony.

These are my reflections, the thoughts in my head, and the information that I walk around with from here to there— my "walking around" attitude. This information is birthed by observation, followed by a pause and a mindful digestion of its parts, and it ends with a choice. Information can ultimately be viewed positively or negatively, and what follows is our attitude, and hence our experience. This is what defines our lives, one experience, thought, and choice at a time. This is the essence of famous psychiatrist and Holocaust survivor Viktor Frankl's famous quote, "Between stimulus and response there is a space, and in that space is our power to choose our response. In our response lies our growth and freedom."

As I've said before, the choice of how we view the world, the daily juggling of our thoughts and emotions, is what forms the basis of experience, beginning to end. And if I've learned the essence of the McCarthy quote from a previous chapter, it's that the information you put in your head is always there in one form or another. Too often in life, the most harmful things outstay their welcome, and the most beautiful things don't stay long enough; they escape the fleeting confines of the here and now—and do so quickly.

REFLECTION 1: THE BEACH

"I was no longer a fragment of the uni-
verse—I was the universe."

- Jim Carey

I waded out into the pristine, emerald waters of the Gulf of Mexico on an average day in June. The sun was shining bright in the noon position overhead, and I was enjoying another day at the beach with my family in Marco Island, Florida. The weather was perfect. As I stood there waist deep, gazing across the calm Gulf waters, I started to get a rather odd feeling. What was odd was that I wasn't feeling at all. I couldn't feel the sand on my feet. I couldn't feel the air. I couldn't feel the sun's rays. And I couldn't feel the water against my skin.

I realized that I was in a profound state of equilibrium, a thermal balance of all the elements: earth, wind, fire, and water. For a brief moment, we were all one. Then, this wave of peace and energy swept across my body like never before—the most noticeable stillness of my life. Everything made sense, and even though I wasn't given any direct answers, I think I understood the purpose and beauty of the universe, which is oneness. I basked in this tranquil state for about two minutes, expressing my gratitude for this tiny place I occupy in the vastness of the cosmos.

Today, I walk with a confidence that we live in a purposeful place, an assurance that God didn't create us to live to die. It became abundantly clear that nature and God were the same, working in eternal harmony with a singular purpose. That two minutes in the ocean also confirmed a long-standing suspicion for me that the concept of death has no rational argument, and it has no dominion. Death had never made sense to me, and certainly not after those two minutes in the oneness of the universe. I will not and cannot accept annihilation. There's no such word. That day in the sea was the day that death died and the day life would go on—forever.

REFLECTION 2: THE QUARTER

"The most dangerous thing in the world
is to get something you didn't earn."

- T.D. Jakes

I opened my locker at the gym and there it was—a quarter. At first, I thought it was a bit odd, this random quarter sitting there. The last person to use the locker took everything out except for that coin? Didn't they see it there? Did they get distracted and simply move on before realizing it was left behind? Nonetheless, I started unpacking my bag and changed into my gym clothes for my workout. I picked up the quarter and placed it in the side pocket of my bag, but as a did, I felt a slight panic, like I had done something wrong. And I had. I'd taken something that wasn't mine. I didn't earn it.

To me, it wasn't about the quarter, and not many people are going to care about losing twenty-five cents. It's not like they lost a bag full of money. No one would think less of me if I picked up that coin and didn't seek out its rightful owner. The lesson was in the personal awareness that the quarter instantly brought forth, that in life, I have to earn everything, including my own happiness. No one is going to do it for me, nor is it their responsibility to do so.

I've been given many opportunities in life. I've gotten pretty lucky. But I asked myself an important question: Do I want to get lucky with my own happiness? Luck, by definition, represents the statistical unlikelihood that a specific event will happen, and I wasn't willing to gamble on my own happiness. But isn't life sort of a gamble? Perhaps, but if we roll the dice enough times, we'll eventually get what we're looking for. Getting lucky is about persistence. Such is also true about our own happiness. We'll never get lucky and just find it in a locker one day. We have to earn it. We have to be persistent in its pursuit.

The quarter represented something deeper for me, that the true value of life, the hardest pursuit any of us will face— the pursuit of happiness—will never be handed to us. It cannot be bought, and it's not something we inherently deserve. It's something we earn through our choices alone. And in anything, even our thoughts themselves, there's always a choice—a good choice, a bad choice, and the right choice. All too often in my life, the good choice and the right choice weren't necessarily the same thing, and so the prayer goes: "Oh God, grant me the wisdom to know the difference."

REFLECTION 3: THE TRIM

"No man, for any considerable period, can wear one face to himself, and another to the multitude, without finally getting bewildered as to which may be the true."

- *Nathaniel Hawthorne, The Scarlet Letter*

One morning during a home improvement project, I was pulling off some old baseboard trim when I came face-to-face with one of life's most basic truths, a revelation that would start to change how I viewed most everything in my life—in particular myself.

Trims come in a variety of shapes and sizes. Some are made of expensive materials, others not. Some trim is attractive to some people, others not, and there's usually a trim style that suits anyone's individual preference. They're designed to bring texture, depth, and contrast to an otherwise formless surface, each with its own personality and intricate combination of carvings and designs—just like each of us.

It became immediately clear that this particular piece of trim had been painted over many times. It was also clear that the original carpenter had paid little or no attention to detail. Big globs of caulk filled in the gaps created by his lack of proper craftsmanship. The white paint was thick against the underlying wood, and there was a series of descending drip lines here and there. Obviously, the last person to paint did so in a hurry and also without much attention to detail. Above all else, I noticed that most of the original detail of the

MEMOIRS OF AN ORDINARY GUY

trim—the original beauty—had been lost through layers and layers of paint and caulk, through a lack of focus and care.

I asked myself why the trim had so much caulk and paint. Maybe it's because the carpenter didn't take enough time with his craft. Maybe the carpenter wasn't trained properly for the task, and instead of starting over and fixing his mistakes—getting it right—he took a shortcut with the caulk and simply filled the gaps. Maybe the painter didn't like to see the imperfections—the old, dirty, and bruised surface. Maybe it was just too hard to clean. Maybe he didn't care, or maybe it was just easier to start over, with a new layer of paint. Now re-read this from a different perspective: You're the carpenter. You're the painter. And you're also the trim.

Keep building *you* the right way, with diligence and attention to detail—to the little things. Don't hide the mistakes and the scars. And if you need to learn something new, do so honestly and with the right intent, and avoid too much paint, because sooner or later you'll cover up the real you—the most beautiful thing of all. And if you can no longer recognize the original trim, strip all the paint off, start over, and repaint with only the thinnest of veneers, one that's as transparent and timeless as the soul itself.

REFLECTION 4: THE NICEST GUY I NEVER MET

"Understand the power of likability."

- Walter Bond

It was Pokémon night at my gym—Lifetime Fitness in Reston, Virginia—and I had just dropped my off my son for the two-hour event. He was super excited, so I was in a good mood too. I also had a great book with me, and I was perfectly content to sit in the gym lobby and catch on some reading. I sat down on the leather sofa just off the main corridor of the gym's main entrance and started to read. A few minutes later, a round, bald gentleman in the distance began walking toward me. Even from twenty to thirty feet, he gave off a gentle and loving aura. He walked softly and had a genuine, kind smile. His eyes were wide, clear, and welcoming.

As he sat down beside me, I could literally feel his presence. He was one of the warmest and softest people I'd ever been around. He brought a sense of peace and calm to the small area we shared and to that otherwise cold and sterile corridor. We exchanged hellos, and it was evident from that simple exchange that he was as likable as he was comforting. I'd simply never been around a nicer human being in my life, yet he was a total stranger who'd I'd known for less than thirty seconds. He was the nicest guy I never met.

He compelled me to ask some of the most important questions of my life. What kind of aura do I give off? Is it an honest reflection of the person inside me? How do people feel when they're around me? Are they as comfortable as I was on Pokémon night? Gosh, I hope so.

REFLECTION 5: THE FIFTH HORSEMAN

> *"I run because I can. When I get tired, I remember those who can't run, what they would give to have this simple gift I take for granted, and I run harder for them."*
>
> *- Anonymous*

It was around mile four when I saw him in the distance. Actually, I saw his walker first. I also saw an older woman walking by his side. She was stoic, erect, and her arms were crossed behind her back, like a drill sergeant at basic training. She was clearly supervising what I assumed was a daily routine. It was odd, different. But what I saw next would forever change my definition of endurance—of real struggle. I've competed in many tests of athletic endurance. I've flirted with my own well-being to cross the finish line, but honestly, I don't think I know what *tired* really feels like. I would learn that lesson on a hot summer afternoon from the most unlikely of teachers—*the Fifth Horseman*.

He was probably ten years old, and his lifeless legs hung between the walker like a couple curtains of thick pasta, and they were just strong enough to provide a momentary pivot—a short reprieve—as he threw his arms and hiked his shoulders into every inch of his journey. His legs swung back and forth with a smooth and predictable rhythm, like the motion of a pendulum inside an antique clock. The walker appeared to be an extension of his hands and arms—an adjunct accessory and a learned necessity, an effective utilization, and a courageous improvisation.

Though he was disabled, he executed his technique with flawless precision—with grace and purpose. It almost looked easy. But as I ran by, the white knuckles of his hands, the bulging veins of his forearms, and (in particular) his face, gave everything away; it was a most unwanted struggle. It was anything but easy, but he was out there giving it his best shot, and over the next couple months I'd see him a dozen more times, doing his similar dance across the asphalt.

This small boy flipped my mindset, a most basic and necessary course correction in my daily attitude. Because of him I now say I *get* to run, not that I have to run; I'm grateful for the opportunity and the ability. Whenever I don't want to run, I think about him, and I run for him. I run for everyone like him—for my mother who's now in a wheelchair of her own. I run harder in their memory, and in the summer of 2020, I added something to my bucket list—my first fifty-mile race. I don't know which race it'll be or when I'll do it, but I'll cross that finish line one day. I'll cross it with the memory of that small boy, because if he can walk one mile, I can certainly run fifty.

REFLECTION 6: THE ANGRIEST WOMAN I NEVER MET

"Two things are infinite: the universe and human stupidity; and I'm not sure about the universe."

- Albert Einstein

It was the dumbest thing I'd ever seen or probably will ever see. I was in line at a local pharmacy when a frazzled, irate woman came in and started berating the woman in front of me. She was furious, and she didn't like it that the woman ahead of me had taken up two spaces in the parking lot outside. I'd seen the event unfold and I agreed; it was a terrible parking job. However, the parking lot was empty. There were easily two hundred spaces available, and the only nuisance the woman ahead of me caused was that she prevented the other woman from parking just six feet closer.

Despite the woman's best explanations or attempts to defuse this other woman's anger, she kept at it. She wouldn't let it go and was making a scene in front of a dozen other customers. More than anything, the woman with the terrible parking skills was dumbfounded—completely befuddled— that this woman was making such a big deal out of something so petty. It was the stupidest argument I'd ever witnessed in my life, and I have my doubts that any in the future will top it. She was the angriest woman I never met.

The lesson I learned, or perhaps the lesson that was rein- forced, is a simple one. It's a chapter from my fictional playbook on life entitled *Just Be Cool*. It's my *Desiderata* and a constant reminder of a behavioral code that I've committed myself to in all things—just play it cool. Light and simple is the way. If I'd had a copy of my unwritten code that day, I would've casually handed it to the angry woman and walked away. I'm not saying it's gospel, but it's served me pretty well so far. It's what I wish someone will tell me when I get out of line. It's direct, explicit, and as honest as I can get. It's what we all want to say. It reads:

> Don't do that. Don't be petty. Don't go out of your way to be a jerk. Don't be a fucking asshole. Don't make your problems somebody else's. If you're having a bad day, fucking deal with it. If you have some real shit going on, I mean real shit, than I'm all ears. I have empathy too. But deal with that in private. Don't lash out at a total stranger. Don't be a pain in the ass. Don't be overly needy, so desperate that you'll do anything for attention, positive or negative. If you're going to pick a fight, pick a good one, one that will improve our general condition. If you're so angry that you have to yell at somebody about a parking space, maybe you should take a long, hard look at something else—yourself. Or maybe you need a long hard dose of something else? Maybe that's been hard for you to find, and perhaps that's the problem. Maybe you should lock yourself in your house until you're ready

to be civil; it would do us all a big favor. Focus on your own shit. Don't worry about what other people are doing. In the grand scheme of things, what does it really matter? If you don't have something nice to say, keep your fucking mouth shut. And if you do have something negative to say, first ask, why do I feel this way? What am I really trying to accomplish here? Then ask, should I say anything at all? You'll find, most often, it's your own problem—your own misguided need—not the person on the receiving end of your dumb ass. Don't complain. But if you do, complain about something that matters, that through its resolution it changes the nature of the world, or it changes someone's life. If you have an opinion about something, offer it seldom. There's a fine line between having an opinion and being opinionated. No one likes the latter. Don't lose your cool. I hate to break it to you, but if you're the first person in an argument to lose their cool, you're probably the loser, in more ways than one. Let your actions and your inactions speak louder than your words. Don't waste your energy and others' with stupid arguments and trivial bullshit. Most negative emotions are a failed opportunity to have positive ones, and negativity is contagious. Negativity is popular. It's a greater pandemic than all others, and we wonder why we're unhappy. I understand that sometimes it can't be avoided. Negative stuff happens, but the choice is always the same—react poorly, react well, or simply not at all.

REFLECTION 7: THE NAIL

"He is risen."

- Matthew 28:6

I'm writing this story on Easter Sunday 2021. I didn't plan it that way, and it seems a bit ironic that I'd be writing about a nail on Easter, one that would resurrect an essential element of my past—a wonderful version of me that I feared was lost: a version of me that was more self-aware than he was confident and more concerned about others' feelings than his own. And while I didn't like some part of myself at every stage of my life (as I wrote about in The Giant), this part I did like, this part I was proud of, and it was the key to living a full life. I considered this quality of mine an art form, of which there are few masters. But I was one of them, a master in the greatest art form of all—that of deeply caring for and loving other people. I'm trying to bring this person back to life, and, if I'm successful, he'll serve me well and enable me to serve others. Though I might not have discovered this version of me had I not found that nail in the middle of the road one random summer day.

I had just finished a short run and was cooling down at a walking pace. Maybe that was fortuitous because had I been moving any faster, I probably would've missed it. I glanced down at the asphalt and noticed a short, stubby nail lying in the middle of the road that could easily puncture a car tire. The first thing that came to mind was that I better pick it up before someone ran over it with their car. I certainly didn't want anyone to step on it, either. I picked it up, looked at it for just a few seconds, and then it hit me like a freight train. The effect of picking up that nail was immediate.

Outside of my family, when was the last time I'd put the concerns of others first? When was the last time I thought about others before I thought about myself? And then it hit me again. Where was that little boy who knew how to care more than he knew how to do anything else? I didn't recognize him anymore. He was nowhere to be found. And, over time, he'd gotten lost—slowly and without my noticing.

When I was a boy, I was a bit of a daydreamer—I still am. There was a space between my thoughts and the real world where I would hang out. I could hear what was going on, but I wasn't really paying attention. I was very present with people one-on-one, but if ever asked in a group setting (where the focus was off me or where my attention wasn't immediately required) what someone had previously said, I'd be in big trouble. This is still a major challenge for me, being a bit lost in the aloofness of a wandering mind. But as a kid, I was hyperaware of one thing—how my words and behavior affected other people. I intimately understood how a careless delivery of words could really hurt another person, even if it was unintentional. After all, what do we remember the most? We remember the things people say, and, most importantly, how they say them.

So I chose my words carefully, and I was extremely mindful of each person I was talking to. Every time I spoke, and with everyone whom I interacted, I'd compile an inventory—a list of things I thought they might be self-conscious about. Maybe this person was overweight, maybe they struggled in school, maybe they weren't very popular, maybe their family didn't have a lot of money, maybe—like me—they didn't have new clothes, or maybe they weren't attractive; the list would go on and on. I'd compile this data quickly, and I'd choose my words accordingly. It was a conscious and deliberate process, one that I felt extremely connected to. In a very basic and innocent sense, the last thing I wanted was to make someone feel bad about themselves or to bring unwanted sorrow or pain into their life—and I could avoid that by carefully choosing what to say.

I'd also avoid drawing any comparisons between myself and another person. I'm not better than anyone, and I didn't want to give anyone that impression either. I rarely talked about myself, and I asked a lot of questions that would keep the emphasis on the other person. And lastly, I feared confrontation, and as such, I was very aware when my interactions turned negative or put me in a position to disagree with someone. I'd rarely, if ever, correct someone in conversation. I was judicious, conservative, hyperaware, and thoughtful with all my words and interactions; hence, I became a good listener. I was likable, popular, and felt genuinely loved by others.

But over time, I found myself taking a smaller and smaller inventory, practicing my craft with less and less focus and attention. That genuine caring and awareness of others seemed to diminish, and I became more self-centered and more selfish as time went on. Did the world take this talent from me, or did I just let it slip? I don't know. Out of necessity—or survival—had I become hardened, jaded, and indifferent? Was it an unintended consequence of being a lifelong introvert, of becoming more introspective as I grew older? Maybe. Maybe that balance between being in the world and out of the world had begun tilting in the wrong direction. But that day I found the nail, I knew the master had left the house long ago. I didn't know when he'd return, but I wanted him back. I knew that a part of me had changed, a beautiful part, a part that needed to be alive once again.

Maybe that's what writing this book is all about, to once again choose my words carefully, a new opportunity to support, encourage, and inspire others through my experiences and through my genuine love for them. Hopefully these words will reach many, and they'll once again reflect my self-professed rank of master—a rank we can all achieve. On this Easter Sunday, let the best parts of you rise up and shine brightly again. Make a deliberate attempt to resurrect them. Find an aspect of yourself that's been lost and restore it to life once more, because it's never too late to become the best version of you—one that's probably been there all along.

These reflections are a part of my playbook, the keys I've found to living a fuller life. They've formed an attitude and mindset that I'm grateful to walk with day-to-day. It's pretty simple really. If I understood that death was not the end (The Beach), if I accepted that happiness is earned through my choices alone (The Quarter), if I found myself through all the layers of paint (The Trim), if I was likable and comforting to others (The Nicest Guy I Never Met), if I could view my struggles with a greater perspective (The Fifth Horseman), if I wasn't an asshole and didn't spend my time and energy doing stupid shit (The Argument), and if I returned to a place where I deeply cared for and loved other people (The Nail), life would probably always be okay; things would always work out for the better. I would find happiness in this life instead of waiting for happiness to find me.

CHAPTER 21

THE DARK FOREST

"To shine your brightest light is to be who you truly are."

- Roy T. Bennett

I n 1950, in New Mexico, on an average day in a cafeteria at Los Alamos National Laboratory, renowned physicist Enrico Fermi was having lunch with several colleagues. When asked the question on the possibility of alien life he famously answered, "Where is everybody?" This answer is now known as the Fermi Paradox. It's the apparent contradiction between the assumed prevalence of intelligent life in the universe and the lack of actual contact with ET. The question is, *why?*

There have been many attempts to explain why we haven't had contact with an alien civilization. Given the age of our universe, currently estimated at 13.8 billion years old, and the size of our galaxy alone—with an estimated four hundred billion (400,000,000,000) stars—it's reasonable to assume that a handful of those stars with habitable planets would've sprung intelligent life and we would've seen or heard from somebody. But we haven't, an almost impossible thing to imagine given the size of the Milky Way. And if this seems improbable, now consider that there are approximately two hundred billion (200,000,000,000) Milky Ways in the known universe. Multiply those two together and that's a really big number, a high probability of life popping up somewhere. At a minimum, we should've picked up a radio signal from somebody, a cosmic "hello" traveling at the speed of light. But no such greeting. Nothing. Zero.

Perhaps intelligent life really is that rare in the universe, perhaps the distances are too great for even light to travel, or perhaps civilizations destroy themselves or others before they're capable of making contact. Worse yet, perhaps one particular alien civilization is so powerful and so advanced that they've colonized the whole galaxy and eliminated all life that's foolish enough to reveal its location. The latter is what has come to be known as the "Dark Forest" theory.

One of my favorite reads is the epic trilogy "Remembrance of Earth's Past" by Cixin Liu. The first book, *The Three-Body Problem*, won the Hugo award in 2015 for best science fiction novel. The story revolves around an impending alien invasion, and what, if anything, the human race can do to prepare itself. In his second book in the series, *The Dark Forest*, Liu writes:

The universe is a dark forest. Every civilization is an armed hunter stalking through the trees like a ghost, gently pushing aside branches that block the path and trying to tread without sound. Even breathing is done with care. The hunter has to be careful, because everywhere in the forest are stealthy hunters like him. If he finds another life—another hunter, angel, or a demon, a delicate infant to tottering old man, a fairy or demigod—there's only one thing he can do: open fire and eliminate them.

It sounds terrifying, a malevolent cadre of hunters lurking in the darkness—that we may be at the mercy and will of an advanced civilization intent on our destruction. Even more terrifying is that this theory would only have to happen once to be proved true, that there's all-powerful monster out there, a cosmic sniper, picking off fledgling civilizations before they can fight back, before they know what hit them. This theory has been used to question programs like the Search for Extra-Terrestrial intelligence (SETI) and sparked public policy debates on the prudence of blasting our signals into interstellar space. Some argue if these signals reach anyone that resembles us, it could be a really bad idea!

For a short while, after finishing the series, this theory fascinated me. Maybe in an odd way it would also be a bit comforting to know there was something out there—a presence, good or bad, gives us hope there's some meaning in the world, some purpose. If we could only make contact, maybe we'd have the chance to ask questions we don't have the answers to; the deeply spiritual and existential questions that continue to haunt us. Or maybe my fascination was a warning, that asking too many questions, getting too removed from one's self, and endlessly searching the cosmos—a place far beyond our true foundation—was literally a dead end. Maybe life is designed to be much simpler than we all give it credit for? Maybe we find the universe only when we find ourselves?

The theory seemed plausible—almost rational—until one ordinary day on just an average run when I received a great gift, an analogy to *The Dark Forest* in everyday life. This experience changed the way I thought about existence itself, the seemingly dark and scary place we call the universe, and our individual lives. By a small little messenger on the side of the road, I was asked a great question: Should I hide or should I shine? As the American poet Dylan Thomas once wrote, should I "go gentle into that good night?" Recently, I was inspired to answer this question with a poem—my first.

The Dark Forest

By Daniel Stuart Olmes

O dark forest, o dark night,
You seem so empty, so absent of light.
Do you hear my cries? Do you hear me roar?
Closed off, closed in, small hints, no door.
I'm naked, I'm cold, so fragile, so weak,
But there's a strength inside me, if only a peek.
Is anyone out there? Can anyone hear?
It's the emptiness and chaos that I o so fear.

I've asked. I've knocked. Found truths and lies,
A lurking presence that I can't deny.
Maybe there's shelter, a place to hide?
But I know it's somewhere that I can't reside.
The ghosts, the demons, they're both the same,
Am I haunted? Or cursed? Two burdens to tame.
A path here, a fork there, a whisper, a flicker,
Danger is upon me, its approach seems quicker.

A watcher? A hunter? A villain? A test?
I'm stumbling, I'm falling, this isn't my best.
Still breathing, still searching, a maze—my mind,
I'm anxious, I'm scared of what I might find.
The darkness, the paths, the branches, the weeds,
Please give me a clue to where it all leads!
I'm lost, I'm tired, my most critical hour,
That's when I saw the most beautiful little flower.

O beautiful flower, my precious new friend,
Tell me your secrets, what advice can you lend?
In the midst of the darkness, what
do your petals reveal?
Teach me your lessons so my soul, too, may heal.
"Fear not," she said. "Shine, baby, shine!
"Reveal your beauty as I've revealed mine.
"Just be you," she said, "and I will be me;
"I've created this little flower for all the world to see."

O dark forest, o dark night,
You're now so full, so colorful, so bright!
I'm not alone, no longer afraid,
It's the law of nature I finally obeyed.
I am the universe, the forest, the light,
I'll give life my fullest, with all my
heart, mind, and might.
I'll never hide. I'll never waver.
The richness of life—the search—I'll savor.

O beautiful flower, you're with me forever.
Your lessons, your presence, these things I'll treasure.
And as I walk through here and tomorrow,
There'll be less pain, less suffering, less sorrow.
It's my nature to shine, not to wither or hide;
It's in this and no other that I shall abide.
Thank you again for lightening the load,
On this thing we call life, the journey, the road.

Just like the flower, it's not in our nature as human beings to hide. We search, we explore, we work hard, we take risks, we make contact, we love, and we're usually rewarded accordingly. Sometimes these things lead to darkness, but like anything, that's our choice—our burden. So shine your brightest for all the world to see. Be yourself, unafraid, regardless of who's watching. Be comforted by little things, even in the midst of the void. And don't go gentle into that good night. Not ever!

Reading a science fiction novel is ordinary. Being temporarily intrigued by a scientific theory about aliens is ordinary. But for both to converge on a little flower on the side of the road on an average spring day and to have it change my view of the universe and my place in it? That's extraordinary.

In the blink of an eye, an ordinary guy turned poet. Maybe that's the signal I was waiting for all along.

CHAPTER 22

THE ROAD

"Two roads diverged in a wood, and I—
I took the one less traveled by,
And that has made all the difference."

- Robert Frost

The scouting combine of the National Football League (NFL) is an annual, week-long event for prospective professional football players. It occurs just before the NFL draft in April and gives coaches and scouts an opportunity to evaluate top players across a series of standard measures—specifically to judge their speed, agility, and strength. It's by invite only—an elite group—and most players participate in five main events: the forty-yard dash, the shuttle run, the vertical jump, the broad jump, and the bench press. The latter is the only measure of physical strength and consists of each player performing as many repetitions of a fixed weight as possible; in this case, 225 pounds. The average total repetitions for a wide receiver or defensive back—players with similar, yet still superior body types to mine—is about fifteen, and for many years I based most of my workouts on progressing toward that goal, toward that universal measure of brute strength. And while most NFL wide receivers and defensive back outweigh me by forty pounds or more, my personal record is eleven repetitions, which is a pretty good number. I was proud of that number. But, in my lifetime, there probably won't be a twelfth, and it's in that twelfth repetition—that point of complete exhaustion—where the gift of running hides her magnificent glory.

What's the significance of that twelfth rep, and how does it have anything to do with running? Well, consider this: that twelfth rep under the bar represents a physical barrier, one that willpower or artificial substances simply can't overcome—a point where you just can't push any more, a point of total physical exhaustion. This barrier reveals itself quickly, and in my case, I reached what felt like a brick wall in about fifteen seconds. Fifteen seconds to perform eleven reps—my personal best. And so I ask the questions: Where is the physical barrier in running? Where is that brick wall? How tired would I have to be—how close to death—that I couldn't take one more step?

The questions continue. How fast and how long can I run? What does a personal best in running look like? How long can my heart power my body? How long can I endure the pain, the struggle? Is it for just fifteen seconds, or for a lifetime? And will I give up? Will I ever stop just so the pain will go away, because I can't handle the struggle? When will I take my last step, and could I have run a little bit harder?

It's in these questions where I found the beauty of running, in its most precious analogies to life itself. And whether it's across seven miles of asphalt or on the actual path we all walk in life, the lessons remain the same—the messages unchanged. There's a timelessness in running, and maybe it was on the road where I learned how to really live.

I've been on the road for fifteen years. I've run countless hours and thousands of miles, and in that time, I've gathered an enormous collection of thoughts, emotions, and experiences. I've danced from one end of the emotional spectrum to the other, seeing as much struggle as I've seen success, seeing as much pain as I've seen power, and seeing as much heaviness as I've seen holiness. There were times when I was weak, and there were times when I was strong, and as often as I was slow, I was also pretty damn fast. To say that I've experienced a range of human emotions on the road would not do them service, and they've all been life-changing in one way or another. In good times and bad, there was always something to learn. There was always an experience worthy of my attention and memory.

I've slowed down at points—it's been hard—but I've always been headed in the right direction. I've always made forward progress and never run backward—even when I was the most tired and in my darkest hours. To quote a great twentieth-century poet, Sylvester Stallone:

> Let me tell you something you already know. The world ain't all sunshine and rainbows. It's a very mean and nasty place, and I don't care how tough you are, it will beat you to your knees and keep you there permanently if you let it. You, me, or nobody is gonna hit as hard as life. But it ain't about how hard ya hit. It's about how hard you can get hit and keep moving forward. How much you can take and keep moving forward.[7]

Life is hard, and so is running. I've run fast, and I've run slow, but I've never stopped. I'll stop when I can't take one more step—when I've reached that twelfth rep. Maybe my personal best—the measure of how good of a runner I was in the end—will be decided on that day I take my last step, which will also be the day I take my last breath. And to quote another great poet, Eminem, I'll run "'till I collapse…until the roof comes off, 'till the lights go out…until my legs give out from underneath me."

Early on in my running career, I came across another quote that now stands above all the rest in this genre, and an obscure runner named Monte Davis phrased it best, as quoted

---

7 Stallone, Sylvester. *Rocky Balboa*. 2006; CA: Metro-Goldwyn-Mayer, Columbia Pictures, Revolution Studios. 102 min.

in his 1976 book *The Joy of Running*. He said, "It's hard to run and feel sorry for yourself at the same time." That quote had always been intriguing, but it's now profound in reflecting on a long career as a runner, and it became clear while writing the final chapter of this book why running is so important to me. I can tell you that it's nearly impossible for me to have a negative emotion on the road. Perhaps running is the ultimate distractor and the consummate teacher.

I've experienced a lot on the road, but, honestly, it's the total and curious absence of two emotions that is the greatest gift of all, and the ultimate lesson was not about what I felt but what I didn't feel—two emotions that simply never came while running. Over time, I'd learn that it's possible to avoid these two emotions in many things. The road and life itself are not all that different, and while they can be such an unfortunate aspect of life, these two emotions didn't need to be a part of mine—or yours either.

Fear is one. I don't fear the road nor any of its inherent dangers. I accept that there will always be potholes—obstacles—and I'll do my best to avoid and overcome them. I'm not afraid that the road will be too hard to run, and deep down, that's how I want it anyway, for there's rarely satisfaction in anything that's easy. I don't avoid the road for fear that I can't run my best, might fail to achieve a goal, or of not living up to someone else's expectations. I'm not afraid that someone else will outrun me, because someone always will. I just run for me and for those who can't run. I run for the experience, but I never run to win, and once I realized this, I learned to discount winning as a measure of my success, happiness, or a reason to be on the road at all. I'll never run a race to tell someone that I did, to brag, or to draw a comparison between myself and others. You'll never see my trophies on the wall.

The road is sometimes crowded, but I'm not afraid there won't be enough room for me. There's room for all of us. I'm not afraid of being judged on the road; it doesn't care what I look like or how fast I am. I don't need to impress the road nor is it necessary to compete for its attention. The only competition is within. The road makes me look skinnier, something that I always feared and felt sorry for myself for, but it's made me stronger in every way—a fact that I now consider with a sense of irony.

I'm not afraid the road will be boring or not satisfying enough, and I won't be picky. It makes no difference what road I'm on, and the more roads I choose and the more I give them my best effort, the easier the next roads become. Any road will do, and there are many. Every road is different, and so is every runner—each built to run a different race. Each runner is of equal value, and we're each given the same task— to choose a good road and to run as fast as we can for as long as we can.

I'm not afraid of running on the opposite side of the road. I want to see what's coming in my direction, and I don't want to get hit in the back, to be blindsided by someone who isn't aware of my presence, or by someone who doesn't have my best intentions at heart. Being on the opposite side of the road can be lonely, particularly with your thoughts and beliefs, but it's an opportunity to see things from a different angle, from different point of view. I also want to see the faces of the people I pass, not their backs. I want to connect with them, to reach them, to wave, to acknowledge their presence, and to momentarily lift their day—if even for a second.

I'm not afraid of running alone, and I crave the solitude, which is sometimes necessary. I'm not afraid that the road will abandon me; it will always be there, and if I leave it for a time, it will patiently wait for me to return. The same is true of the people we love, and of those that love us. That connection is never broken; no time is too long.

The road doesn't pay me to run, nor do I expect it to. I don't expect wealth or riches along the road, and I'm not afraid the road won't pay enough dividends. I run hard, faster than most, but that doesn't mean I deserve something special. The road usually rewards hard work, and it gives many treasures, the kind that aren't for sale. And what makes every road worth running is what we ultimately learn—the strength and confidence it develops and the truths that it reveals along the way. The real gifts.

I'm not afraid of running in bad weather, nor does it ever make me uncomfortable. Cold, rain, heat, wind, darkness, I

MEMOIRS OF AN ORDINARY GUY

love it all. Perhaps the greatest lesson in running—in endurance sports—is that you need to get comfortable being uncomfortable, and the same is true about life. It's about weathering the storm, and when I see one coming, I usually run faster to avoid it, or when the rains do fall, they cool me down, offering a momentary reprieve from my efforts, a break to reset and regain my strength. And when the rains fall too hard, I have faith that there will always be someone there to help, to offer a hand—even the outreach of a total stranger. There's always a storm somewhere on the road, but most times it's in our own head. Our experience in the end is the attitude we bring to that storm and to the things we experience. An anonymous writer said it best: "The devil whispers, 'You cannot withstand the storm.' The warrior replies 'I am the storm!'"

I'm not afraid of a new road, one that I haven't run before, and I'll eagerly await what's around every corner. I'll let this road come to me instead of insisting on a sign—a guidepost—to assure me of what's ahead. I'm not afraid of taking a wrong turn or getting lost, and I'm confident I'll always find my way home. I have faith in the road, and I have faith in myself. My technique is sound, and I've prepared properly. I like to tell myself that I'm strong enough for anything—and time will tell. Hopefully, my strength will never give out and I'll always give the road my best shot. If not, tomorrow will be another opportunity to run faster, to get stronger. I'm not afraid of getting sick or that I'll get injured and be unable to finish the race. The road will never end, even after I take my last step. It has a purpose. It leads somewhere, and along the road there will always a better version of me. Maybe on the next road I'll have wings to fly.

Fear is the first. Regret is the second. I've never finished a run and regretted being on the road. I've never said to myself, "Gosh, I wish I hadn't done that." Even the worst runs made me feel better—clearer, calmer, and more fulfilled. Even the worst runs taught me something. If I made a mistake or failed to achieve a goal or had a bad attitude, there was always tomorrow. I never lamented on the bad runs I've had in the past, because there was always a positive lesson in each of them—a lesson learned. A run was always an opportunity to see something new and beautiful and to see the little things that passed by—to be inspired by the goodness of the world. The road is where I've tried to perfect the art of observation, so I can always be keenly aware of every good thing around me.

I've never regretted not running more, and it's important for me to find balance, one that's in harmony with the other roads I'm on. I don't want to be a great runner at the expense of being a great father, a great husband, or a great friend. I've never regretted the hours of dedication to the road, or, in all honesty, the hours of dedication to myself and to my physical and spiritual health. If these two aren't given the proper attention, I believe all else will suffer. The road is my temple. It's where I find the secrets of the sages and an attitude for the ages. It's where I find the truest gifts in life: peace, love, happiness, and the courage and strength to achieve the highest of arts—the eternal progression of my being. The road is tough, but I promise you, the fight is your friend.

It's amazing what you can see when you're not focused on the negative, when it becomes something you just can't do. The road is a personal sanctuary, one that provides a short pause from the things that plague us most: fear, regret, and the combination of these two, which is negativity. And why is that? Maybe it's because negativity takes away the gift of the present moment, a place where the greatest treasures and beauties of our world exist. The present is the continuous creator of our past, and, if viewed differently, it can create a different history, and thus, a better experience of the world, beginning to end.

In the end, the road showed me a different world from the one I thought I lived in. It led to a shift in my mindset and has provided a new path, one marked by strength, optimism, and a newfound perspective on almost everything. The road has helped reveal the positive nature in most things, even amidst the difficulties and tribulations we all face in our lives. On the road, I view life through a different lens that allows me to see the real beauty around me and to observe my thoughts and emotions in a different way, without fear or worry. Running is a fountain of inspiration, a spring that never runs dry.

On the road, I found that I'm surrounded with beauty and love every day, and I can translate the experience of running into everything else in my life. I discovered that I'm my fastest when I let love be my driving force, and negativity slows me down. I found that negative emotions are most times a choice—something I had control over—and they had no usefulness in my life. I learned that it was okay to slow down, to walk, and to catch my breath, but it was never okay to stop.

In one way or another, everyone is a runner, and there are many roads out there—a road for everyone. Find yours. Let it be a safe haven for your heart and mind. Let it distract you from the all the negative things in your life, and you'll be amazed what you find. The road helped me discover so many things I didn't know were there, and I probably couldn't have written this book if it weren't for the road—one I decided to run a little differently. And that has made all the difference.

In closing, I'd like to share one of my favorite quotes from a most unlikely teacher, Agent K (Tommy Lee Jones) from the movie *Men in Black*. If you haven't seen the movie, the Men in Black are agents in a top-secret government organization that monitors the existence of an extra-terrestrial presence on Earth—one that's completely unknown to the general public. Sitting on a park bench in Lower Manhattan in the shadow of the Stature of Liberty and trying to recruit his future partner played by Will Smith, Agent K says: "1,500 years ago, everybody knew that the Earth was the center of the universe. 500

years ago, everybody knew that the Earth was flat. And fifteen minutes ago, you knew that people were alone on this planet. Imagine what you'll know tomorrow."

To me, this quote is about much more than the scientific theories that have been disproven over time or about being among a select few who are in the know (the Men in Black). It testifies to the simple truth that sometimes we need to challenge what we think we know—or perhaps what we believe—and to view tomorrow with a renewed curiosity and passion. It's never too late to start the learning process all over again, and it's never too late to experience the world a little differently. It's a testament to the fact that it's possible for an ordinary guy like me to find extraordinary beauty every day of his life, and it's never too late to find the things that are really worth knowing, which are usually the experiences that are grounded in human love—the everyday experiences that changed my life.

Silence the negativity. Loosen your jaw and take a step back. Never be afraid to run on a different road. And, above all, watch with glittering eyes the whole world around you, because the magic is out there, patiently waiting for its ultimate reveal. All I can say is that it worked for me, and it's worth repeating. Imagine what you'll know...*tomorrow*.

AFTERWORD

'm sitting here in a Ford dealership in Northern Virginia waiting on a service for my F-150 pickup. Yes, I've taken my truck to the dealership for an oil change. I'm embarrassed to admit that I have a truck and don't change my own oil. But sometimes, there just isn't enough time, and the convenience is well worth it. Plus, the short respite is providing an opportunity to write this afterword—to provide a summary statement and some concluding thoughts to my book. To say it is inspired and in-the-moment is an understatement (I wrote this in twenty minutes start to finish). So, with tears in my eyes, lips pursed, and a surging energy in my heart, here we go.

Let me again say thank you. Thank you for the time you've taken to read this book. I'm grateful beyond words, and I hope walking you through some of my journey was worth it to you. Maybe some of it was familiar? I hope that's the case. Because it's the journey we're all on. In that sense, we're all connected.

Life's a miracle. You're a miracle! And as such, always be mindful of what's right in front of you in every moment. You never know who might walk by in a dingy parking garage on just an average day. That person could change everything. It could be a subtle, yet glorious event that changes how you view the world. It could be what turns the ordinary into the extraordinary. And pay attention to your dreams, because sometimes they might not be what you think. They might be a warning hiding in the shadows of your subconscious. They might be telling the greatest truths of all—the real you, telling you something you need to hear.

Follow the yellow brick road but only for so long. The yellow brick road is a road we all walk at some point, and there's an important lesson to be learned in the pursuit of God, whatever that means to you. But follow your intuition too. Look in new and different places for ultimate truths. I believe we're all looking for the "man behind the curtain," but he might not be at the end of the yellow brick road. He might be the "Tiny Dancer" in your car one warm summer night.

Keep your heart and mind open to the signs and symbols in your life, whether it's a dancing rainbow on your worst day or a blade of grass dancing in a gentle breeze, for they both dance the same dance. They're both equally beautiful, and they're both a product of the imagination of God. The trick is to see the spirit and timelessness of both, equally. In the end, they're just different manifestations of the same thing, the ultimate power and wonder of the universe—which I've found to be God's equal, one in the same.

Find the strength and inspiration of children, especially those with crippling disease. They seem to smile more than we do, and they're a powerful reminder of just how strong we can be, for their attitude and wisdom is beyond their years and beyond words—ineffable. Don't be afraid of a new and unique relationship. It might be an inconvenience or require some time and energy, but there was also a time when you needed someone, and no one should stand alone at a cold, rainy bus stop.

Be great for someone or something. You never know the impact you might have on someone—how the butterfly's wings might affect the weather a thousand miles away. And certainly don't complain because—let's be honest with ourselves—we rarely have a legitimate reason to do so. Have reasonable expectations of the world and of life, and pick someone up and carry them forward with you. Not everyone is as strong as you are. This is probably the greatest service of all.

We're all tired sometimes, but just remember there are some people who are *always* tired. Maybe one day you'll see a flicker in the distance that'll change your life, a reminder that maybe you're not actually *that* tired, a reminder of what you're really capable of when you find the will to fight on. Be an ambassador for the human race, a beacon for the light we have, not the darkness. Be an example of all that's wonderful in the world and find your pearl, the one thing you'll cherish above everything else. I guarantee it'll be love in the end, whether in the form of a child, a partner, a friend, or just a total stranger. It's the unifying force of all there is. It's the language of God. There's no greater truth than this.

Keep your eyes open in the darkness. You never know what you might see. It might change everything, even in your darkest hour. There are four horses you'll ride to self-destruction, and maybe more, but this is necessary. The four horsemen are a metaphor for me, and they're the most real lessons I've ever learned. Find them. Understand them. And become a greater version of you. The only way I found happiness was to live the lives I didn't want and to be the man I didn't want to be—a useful and profound paradox for living. The four horsemen brought the death of everything that needed to change in my life and directed a rebuilding of everything I knew I could become.

Don't drink the Coke. It tastes good, but be patient and let others have an opportunity first because there's always someone who needs it more. Be a leader not a taker. Think of others first. Don't be afraid to miss your mark or fail to achieve a goal. This might teach you the greatest lesson of all. It might help you refocus on what's really important— to be true to yourself. And remember this, and it's true anywhere—in sports, at work, with your faith, with self-improvement, in relationships, and really with anything that's worth a damn—hard work always wins. And if hard work doesn't win the first time, it's the failure—the loss—that motivates the second, third, fourth, or however many times it takes for you to achieve your goal. It's actually failure that's the greatest teacher—the greatest motivator—and the satisfaction in knowing that you gave life everything you had, that's timeless and that's what you'll remember. And also remember this—relationships matter, they matter more than most things.

Life's a puzzle with a lot of pieces. It's hard, sometimes frustrating, and it takes a long time to complete. But that's the point. It's a worthy and virtuous endeavor, and we never have to do it alone. And in this endeavor, we're given an instrument to play—in my story, a drum. Each one is unique. Each one has a different shape and size and makes a different sound, but they're all equally beautiful. And our task is the same, to play the best we can, for as long as we can. Whoever you play your drum for, just remember this: play it loud! Play it loud enough so that everyone will hear it one day.

Make meaningful connections to people. They could be a Marine lieutenant, a security guard at a train station, a refugee in a photograph, a young man in a coffee shop, a flirtatious woman in an elevator, a random guy eating breakfast, or two bodyguards. They might just be the greatest teachers of your life. And reflect on everything—even simple things—whether it's a fleeting moment at the beach, a quarter you find in a locker, a piece of wood trim, good people, bad people, or a rusty nail in the middle of the road. Give these things a little more time and attention. They, too, can be great teachers if you let them.

Shine your brightest in the dark forest we call life, because who gives a shit who's watching, honestly? There's no cozy little spot in the world, no place to hide. And hiding is not in our nature anyway. And don't ever give up. Don't ever stop living. Keep your eyes open and enjoy the ride. You're on the road for a reason, and it can bring you more love and happiness than you can ever imagine. Just keep fucking running!

- Danny

December 16, 2021

ACKNOWLEDGMENTS

'd like to thank the following people who inspired or directly assisted me in the writing of this book. I cannot adequately express my gratitude for your love, support, and positive and constructive feedback. So many aspects of this book would not be the same without you. With all my heart, thank you!

First and foremost, I'd like to thank my family—my wife Elisa and my two children, Chase and Berkeley, my father and stepmother, my mother, my aunt Barbie, my cousin Brian, and my cousin Michael. I'd like to thank Anthony Ziccardi and Heather King of Post Hill Press for publishing this work. This book would not have come into the world without you and I'm eternally grateful for the opportunity you gave me as a first-time author. Many thanks to my editor and trusted advisor Chuck Cascio, to my friend and advisor Leti Gomez, and to my graphic designer Jacy Richardson. You were an integral part of my journey.

I'd like to also thank my friends Jamie Clarke, Debbie Strauss, Dave Frandano, Paul Vogelzang, Miles Sabrick,

Jonathan Widdifield, Bob Barker, Kia Barker, Pinky Bellino, Alice Quan, Bridge Littleton, Stephen Scardamalia, Matt Tracy, Corrine Nickell, John Costello, Linda Koretz, Brittany Holzmacher, Matt Buchanan, Kendall Vitale, Mark Drever, Jared Greer, Ethan Kennedy, Brody Buhler, Laura Siegel, Greg Staufer, Steven Caplin, Nate Coughran, Brian Diemar, Jess Thompson, Josh Mazon, Dean Carver, Patty and Scott Carpenter, Lance Leggitt, Ella Kaulback, Paul Blanchard, Monika Nielsen, Greg Bloom, Larry Sullivan, Mary Arnhold, Paul Kashchy, Maura Clos, Brian Donohue, Dave Richardson, Steve Kramer, Gale Nemec, Len Shapiro, TJ Doremus, Ralph Denino, Bob Nelson, Jared Munyan, Mike Olsen, Courtney Wirwahn, Talai Johansen, Cliff Song, Sara Phillips, Jenny Long, Scott Montgomery, Zella Mansson, Dak Hardwick, Tom Dolan, Trine Bietz, and Miranda Devine. I love you all!

ABOUT THE AUTHOR

Daniel Stuart Olmes is a husband, father of twins, entrepreneur, and Aerospace and Defense executive residing outside of Washington, D.C., in the Northern Virginia suburbs. He is currently the president and chief operating officer of a mid-sized government contractor and is an avid reader, runner, and volunteer, spending most of his time on the baseball field as a Little League coach. He has founded two companies—Middleburg Capital and Hellen Systems—the first being a commercial real estate investment firm, and the second, a technology company focused on a national security initiative to create a ground-based back-up for the Global Positioning System (GPS). He earned a bachelor's degree in biology at Virginia Tech in 2000.

Jamie Clarke has seen teams from the inside and the outside: Olympic teams, NHL teams, sales teams, and start-up teams. What connects them all is pressure—external or self-imposed. With his own hard-won philosophy of risk management—and a storytelling technique that can take you from laughter to tears in minutes—Jamie leaves it all on stage.

He recharges audiences with a new perspective on success or failure, and risk or reward, with strategies for tackling obstacles to reach new levels of success. You can learn more at his website: https://jamieclarke.com/